SELF-ASSEMBLY

VICTORIA LOMBARDI

DEDICATION

To my people—to the ones who have stuck by me through it all. To those who believe in my purpose and in the power of my existence. Thank you for inspiring me to write these pieces. For believing in me when I did not believe in myself and for encouraging me to share my story. You are all a part of this journey and undoubtedly instrumental in my success.

AUTHOR NOTE

Before you move into this collection, make sure you have a pen and a notebook ready. Writing down your thoughts, even in the margins of these pages, will be fundamental to staying engaged and committed to your own growth.

I am here for you, rooting for you, as you move through the five phases of your self-assembly.
— **Victoria Lombardi**

CONTENTS

INTRODUCTION

Self-assembly: *"a process in which a disordered system of pre-existing components forms an organized structure or pattern as a consequence of specific, local interactions among the components themselves, without external direction"* (Oxford Languages).

I want you to know that the contents of this book are written from the deepest parts of my soul. A product of the lessons I have taught myself about life, and the (several) ones I have learned the hard way. This collection is, in turn, for you because it will encourage you to lean into the unknown. It is for you because it will inspire you to stop losing battles by convincing yourself that you are incapable of change. It is for you because it will empower you to awaken your truest self, live in accordance with your principles, and invest in your best interests *first.*

It is for you because it will help you realize that assembling your ideal self begins the day you consciously make an effort to do so.

It will teach you that this very day is the first day you become a free woman.

Making sense of who you are is not the equivalent of accepting yourself for who you have become, or for what society says you have become. The parts of you that are not compatible with your vision—the ones that feel oddly out of place, sharp to the touch, sour in taste, and uneasy within your soul—are not meant for you. Whether it is the condescending partner you constantly appease, the labels you absorb, or the personality traits you despise, you know these things are not meant for you because of their heaviness.

Before you ascribe eternal meaning to these disordered parts and allow them to define your existence, I hope you give yourself permission to **evolve**.

I hope you give yourself time to engage in genuine self-reflection. I hope you lay a strong, well-educated foundation that can support your success. I hope you build and install routines, systems, and patterns that bring out the best in you. And I hope you polish yourself with assets that are compatible with your values, thereby bringing you closer to your most authentic self than you have ever been before.

Know that connecting with yourself in this raw, deeply personal manner pushes you to organize your dysfunction. To weed through the unhealthy habits, the undesired thoughts, and the strangers living rent-free inside your head. As you categorize which components you wish to better integrate into your life—and which to scrap completely—you will form a stronger bond with the core of who you *are*.

You will naturally aspire to transform because these moments will lead you to unearth the latent potential lodged deep within you. They will encourage you to establish structure from the unstructured. They will call on you to sort out the jumbled puzzle pieces floating through your mind and reclaim your inner voice.

This phenomenon derives from the natural human biological process of homeostasis—the one that demands your body maintain balance at all costs. This process endures regardless of any external direction or nudges.

So in case you need a reminder today, your body will always find its way back home. Back to center. **Back to your highest self.**

PART 1
Authorizing

STARTING AGAIN

S tarting this self-assembly does not mean you are a failure. Or a mistake, a lost cause, or a waste of somebody else's time. Rid these words from your vocabulary. **Please.**

As much as the world may lead you to believe that there is something wrong with you, *there is not*. You are just pure water waiting to escape the dam that has been holding you back and gush your way downstream.

Wanting to help yourself—to improve yourself—may mean that there is unrest within your soul. That parts of you do not align with your values, intentions, or current identity. In no way, shape, or form, however, does this mean that there is something *wrong* with you. It is just that these components no longer fit into the organization you set as standard for yourself.

It could be that maybe you hold on to aspects of your existence for far longer than you should because you dread letting go. Maybe you are desperate to reinvent yourself not because there is something *wrong* with you, but because you know there is something more captivating lying within you.

As you spring into action, remember that improvements do not invalidate the core of who you have always been. They simply allow you to shine in a way that better represents who you are today. **They augment what already exists within you and refurbish facets that no longer benefit you.**

THE DECISION

As much as your current system—your body—may feel disordered, harmony and organization are well within reach so long as you believe they are.

It all starts and ends in your own mind.

No outside director, loved one, or influencer is going to get you to where you want to be unless you truly want it for yourself. Building a home you are proud of takes time, but that is what makes the process you are embarking on so rewarding and precious.

Know that change undoubtedly means getting honest with yourself. It means laying bare all your insecurities and putting in the hard work to satisfy your dreams. Your aspirations may sound appealing, but fulfilling them means taking the time to set a proper foundation, build and install a purposeful framework, and trust yourself. These acts will be the ultimate test of your dedication to your assemblage.

Most of all, this construction process teaches you to become friendly with fear, strengthen your inner narrative, and unconditionally live out your highest existence.

If you are toying with the idea of falling into the unknown, I hope you remind yourself that you are the only person who is going to make sense of your soul. If you are not willing to do what is necessary to save yourself, *what makes you think transformation is practical?*

AREN'T YOU TIRED?

You must be so tired.

Aren't you tired of wasting time, fantasizing about a life you are not actually living?

Aren't you tired of hating yourself?

Of holding yourself back in conversations because you do not think you have anything substantial to offer?

What about falling victim to the uninvited guests drifting around your mind?

Aren't you tired of lying awake at night wishing you had a different job or a different body? Of feeling ashamed of yourself, of rolling your eyes every time you look in a mirror?

Aren't you fed up with feeling unsatisfied with your weekdays and living for the weekends?

Aren't you done with letting other people govern your behavior and self-worth?

Aren't you tired of criticizing yourself, of obsessively counting calories, overexercising, and spending all your money on partying, skin-tight bodysuits, and shots at the bar?

Aren't you tired of having no sense of direction, of hoping it all works out but not putting in the effort needed for it to actually work out the way you want it to?

Most of all, aren't you tired of not living up to your potential?

Because if I were you, I would be. I would be because I once was where you are today. *What a tiring place that was.*

THE ITCH

I f you are uncertain about which components will integrate into the highest version of yourself, I want you to ask yourself one question: *what fuels your fire in the morning?*

When you first wake up and the day has hardly begun, and the birds are chirping a springtime song, what calls you?

Is it the thought of consistently pursuing your dreams of becoming a writer, a business owner, a professional athlete, a teacher, or a world leader? Or is it practicing piano, cooking your favorite meal, or rehearsing with your castmates?

Whatever stirs your curiosity and ignites your soul, I hope you choose to run after it. **Do not walk.** Do not let barriers prevent you from chasing your passions. Give yourself the consent you need to closely assess which components are worth keeping in your life, and which are not.

Align your soul with a narrative that keeps you itching to start your day. To thrust out of your cozy bed, push open your windows, and live life to the fullest extent.

TIME IS UP

Recognize that it is time to act. **It is time to act now.**

There is no moment like the present moment because nothing but the present exists, and the longer you wait, the more time passes that you could have dedicated towards your ambitions.

Remember that your time on earth is your most limited resource and that regret is a cold, cold wave that caves in on you when you know you failed to move. Fearing that whatever you have planned for yourself is going to take too long, or be too time-consuming, different, or painful is exactly what keeps you stuck. The clock keeps ticking irrespective of your actions, and you only have one shot to live the life you know you are meant to live.

That is why the last thing you want to do is look back two years from now and wonder what your relationship with yourself would look like if only you had started *then*. If only you had signed up for that class, launched your blog, or broken up with the person you know is not good for you.

Since there is no such thing as a wrong path, making a firm decision is even more necessary. Every single decision you make leads you to another, and to another, and then to another. Despite all the long-term strategizing and playbook writing you do, life works in ways you cannot possibly predict. Everything happens for you, *for a reason*, so stop worrying so much and sending yourself into a tailspin instead of acting on your ideas.

Quit standing in your own way and allow yourself to walk across the starting line. Move up, move on, move out, move past… whatever it takes. *Just move.*

FEARLESS

B e **fearless.** Be without fear. Rid yourself of the voice on your shoulder that constantly tells you that you are not good enough.

- That you do not have what it takes to be successful, so you will fail right from the start.

- That you will never get what you want.

- And that you are meant to keep running in circles and staying unhappy because unhappiness is the only place you feel at home.

- Stop telling yourself that you are selfish for chasing your dreams.

- That you are never going to adjust because you are incapable of surviving without him.

- That you would be better off staying in that toxic partnership because it is all you have ever known.

- Please get rid of the idea that you will embarrass yourself by posting that video you have been dreaming of uploading.

- That you are not *that* girl. That you cannot compete with that girl's looks. Or with her clothes, her wealth, or her personality.

- That you are never going to get the job anyway, so filling out the application is meaningless. They are just going through the motions, and you are out of contention.

- **It is too hard.**

- Quit getting strung up on the idea that it is going to take you years to complete that advanced certificate.

- That trying a new routine, fitness class, dinner recipe, hobby, or book is pointless because you are helpless anyway.

Fear is paralyzing and demonizing. Look out for fear in your thought patterns and comments. Be brave and run as far away from fear-based thinking as humanly possible.

PROMISES

Maybe it is time to promise yourself that you are going to make yourself happy.

That you have what it takes and that no one can influence you to do otherwise. Even on the stormy, ominously dark days, promise to see the silver lining. Promise yourself that no award, fellow human, or degree is worth more than the feeling of joy you derive from *within*. No matter what roadblocks stand between the person in the mirror and the person smiling back at you five years from now, promise to stay consistent. To move forward despite the difficulties life will inevitably throw your way.

No matter what, **promise yourself that *your* happiness comes first.** That walking away from the mindset that no longer serves you, or the lifestyle that leaves you in tears on Saturday night, curled up in a ball rocking back and forth, only catapults your growth.

BUTTERFLY

I f I could only use one word to describe you, it would be **butterfly**.

A seemingly gentle being with so much might, you could knock your way through any restraints. Your strong, colorful wings have carried you through some of the most difficult battles of your young life. You have had your share of rough days and disputed your worth more than you would like to admit.

It has been an uphill battle, with branches, storm clouds, and mud piles obstructing your path. Some days you have contemplated giving up, but that is not you.

You are not willing to sabotage your own existence. You are ready to evolve from the all-too-familiar cocoon you tuck yourself inside of each night. The days of feeling fed up are over, mainly because you have said so. You are willing to stand tall and confidently transcend.

As you embark on your internal metamorphosis, you forge ahead with conviction—aware that you can steer through gusty winds and survive lightning storms. Graceful and beautiful, you glide past rainy days with unmatched poise and dedication. It is not always sunny, but you are always willing to rise and try, try, try again. Most of all, you know your flight will mean sacrificing old ways in place of the unknown. *You see this as a gift, not as a penalty.*

You are a butterfly in every sense of the word. Courageous. Inspiring. Bold. YOU.

ONE DAY

If there is one phrase you need to eradicate from your dictionary, it is *"one day."*

One day I will love myself.

One day I will be happy.

One day I will block out the chatter and address my body image issues.

One day I will have a career I genuinely enjoy, a partner who sees me for who I am, and a home I feel comfortable retreating to every night.

But not today.

Because today, I am not worthy.

I do not have the energy for that today. I am too tired today. I do not have it in me today.

I have an appointment, a conference call, a credit card bill, a dinner date today.

I do not have the time to do that today because it is not in my planner.

Know that there is always going to be something, **it is just whether that *something* is worth sacrificing for your *other* something.**

If you want to escape the cycle of one day—because you need to if you want to truly evolve—you will have to learn to prioritize. To accept the opportunity cost implicit in starting today. It is not easy, but it is the decision you must make if you want to experience sustainable growth.

LOOKING BACK

Leave the relationship and stop looking back.

Leave the friendship and stop looking back.

Leave the university and stop looking back.

Leave the desk job and stop looking back.

Leave your hometown and stop looking back.

Give in to the unknown.

Leave what needs to be left in the past, *in the past*.

You know what no longer brings you happiness and peace of mind. You know when it is time to cut ties and run after your dreams at full speed. **You know when it is time to be free.**

So please stop looking back, dissecting your strategy, and wondering what you could have done better. You only have one shot, and if you do not learn to be okay with the outcome—for better, or for worse—you will continue haunting yourself.

Release the pressure, leave, and stop looking back.

THE CHANCE

E very day you are presented with a chance.

With a new opportunity to advance. To pull yourself from the darkness and build up your tanking self-esteem. A chance to take your supplements, finish that fifteen-minute at-home workout before class starts, and listen to a new episode of your favorite podcast. An opportunity to say *"so long"* to the friends who bring out the worst in you, and to say *"yes"* to that two-month retreat in the desert.

You are given the ability to revise the narrative you have been telling yourself about how terrible your life is. About how you are the victim of your life's circumstances, and you will never find a way out because you have been cursed from the day you were born. *A hopeless, helpless body floating through an awful life.*

Today, you are presented with the chance to tell yourself that the only way out is through.

That the version of your life you play on repeat in your mind is the only one that seems viable because it is the only one you have ever known. And that until you force your mind to skip a beat, that tune will spin over and over and over again. **It will remain all you will ever know.** Only after you overhaul this song's regime—and force it to stop playing—will you confront your dysfunction. It is only then that you will be in control.

When you wake up in the morning, remind yourself that you have a fresh slate ahead of you. The birds are chirping, the sun is glistening, and you are here on this earth for a reason. **Find that reason, fall in love with it, and live it out to the fullest extent.**

ROCK BOTTOM

If there is one thing rock bottom teaches you, it is that you **never want to feel whatever you are feeling again**. Thus, rock bottom is not a place to fear, but a place to embrace.

It is the beginning of a new chapter. It is the wake-up call you so alarmingly resent, but desperately need. The pit in your stomach so disparaging, it provides you with unparalleled motivation to evolve.

At the same time, however, rock bottom cannot be planned for. **It just hits you.**

It creeps up on you on a normal day during a normal task. Normal, that is, for how you have been carrying yourself through life. You are cooking eggs on a rainy Sunday morning after a tough work week and suddenly, it hits you. Your dangerous habits, lack of self-care, dwindling confidence, and unhealthy diet all compound after months and months—even years—of accumulation, to the point you are completely fed up and cannot accept going another second the way you are now.

Humans are hardwired to resist change, though. They will rarely change unless enacting said change is the sole route to survival. Once you tap into this biological element, you will know that there is no other way out except putting in the work.

Get comfortable with who you are and figure out what makes you tick. Take care of yourself all the time (not just when you need it most). Prove to yourself that rock bottom is not an end, but a launching point. **A launching point that sends you into space to glow amongst the brightest stars.**

PERMIT

Once you give yourself permission to set the foundation for your existence, you trigger a string of events that bring you closer to where you need to be.

Making the decision to alter customs that no longer serve you prompts action. It brings you one step closer to achieving your dreams by encouraging you to flee the mind games that keep you locked in the endless cycle of what-ifs, uncertainties, and question marks. Instead of lying awake at night wishing you had it all figured out, you simply start. You start where you are today because you think about where you will be in two weeks, a month, three months, and six months from now if you start **today**.

Your foundation—along with the work you do to prime, build, and install your highest self—will set the pace for a fruitful, meaningful transformation. It will bring you to a place where you no longer avoid inner disturbances, and do not structure your life around the avoidance of pain by remaining overly sensitive towards your behaviors and appearances.

Please do not underestimate the power of getting started today. **Of giving yourself the authorization you need to start today.**

SELF-COMPASSION

S elf-compassion is most crucial on the days when you do not feel motivated to show up.

It is the practice of comforting yourself when you feel low, inadequate, and unlovable. It is treating yourself the same way you would treat the one you love most on a tough day. It is rewarding yourself with that meal you have been craving, letting yourself sleep in when you know you need an extra hour, and forgiving yourself for dropping the ball on your assignment.

Having compassion for yourself is not pitying yourself for being *"poor me."*

It is actively *choosing* to be human. To feel your emotions, but to not let them overtake you. It is stopping critics from blasting a megaphone in your head and making you feel worthless (which only destroys your equilibrium). It is having an optimistic viewpoint, holding your own hands on the nights you feel lost, and reminding yourself it will be alright. It is remembering not to hyperfocus on your progress every single day because you know this will only lead to frustration.

Quit beating yourself up and scouring your self-esteem before you give yourself the chance to shine. There are too many people in this world with bitter hearts, and they are ready to tear you down with their keyboards.

Do not let yourself be the leader of your own hate club.

AFFIRMATIONS

Affirmations to repeat each morning as soon as you wake up, and each night before you fall asleep:

1. I am worthy of experiencing happiness.

2. I am lucky to see another day on this earth, with the freedom to become whoever I want to be.

3. I attract goodness because I radiate goodness.

4. I can educate myself using free resources.

5. I am in control of what I am in control of—nothing else can be stressed over.

6. Pivoting is not the same thing as failing. I can change courses as many times as I see fit.

7. I am stronger than I think I am.

8. I accept myself for who I am today, knowing that I am still a work in progress.

9. I am full of *unfulfilled* potential.

10. The love, acceptance, and inspiration I seek already dwell inside of me.

11. I am my own greatest investment.

12. I have learned from my mistakes, and I forgive myself for not knowing better in the past.

13. I possess the power to savor the present moment.

14. I know my value in this world and will dedicate myself to living out my purpose, no matter what it takes.

15. I am more than enough, and anyone who tells me otherwise is simply not right for me.

16. Oftentimes the hardest battles are the ones I gain the most from, so I am always up for the challenge.

17. My self-confidence cannot be defined by what others think of me.

GOLDEN TICKET

The ticket you give yourself to actively pursue your dream life is priceless. Even though it can feel scary and uncertain, that golden ticket is often the final push you need to actualize your potential. Your official authorization letter to build yourself up and escape the shackles binding you to people, places, and things that make you feel complacent.

Once you release the ties holding you stagnant in the waiting room of life, you expose yourself to a breadth of endless possibilities. To a world in which your vision is fully aligned with your identity, thereby permitting you to serve as a beacon of hope in your community. It is in this place where your apprehension towards living out your purpose fades into a blurry horizon marked by insecurity and resistance.

It is only with this newfound courage that you can forge ahead, let the shadows fall behind you, and emerge from the darkness. *Golden.*

OWNERSHIP

You must speak, and you must speak with purpose. Take initiative over your destiny. No amount of passion, desire, or talk will get you from where you are today to where you want to be unless you *own* your actions. Know that while this may seem overwhelming, it is the little habits that add up to surpass the big ones.

It is how you wake up in the morning—whether you consistently set your alarm clock fifteen minutes earlier so you can meditate.

Who you choose to hang out with and how those people influence you.

It is the extra two seconds you take to put out your vitamins for tomorrow morning.

Electing to be the bigger person instead of posting spiteful comments online.

The way you think of yourself when you catch your reflection.

The stories you tell yourself about who you are and what your capacity is.

It is taking ten minutes to call your Nonnie and catch up with her because she lives alone, and you want her to know how much you love her.

It is remembering to apply moisturizer after your shower, boiling a cup of hot lemon water, and setting limits on your screen time.

Dressing in clothes that make you feel confident instead of trying to keep up with trends that do not suit your style.

Staying mindful of the thoughts passing through your conscious, filtering out unkind comments and not letting hate fester within your soul.

Make the shifts you need to survive today because **these habits compounded over time will be a true testament to your owner-ship over your own life.**

MASTERPIECE

I hope you choose to be graceful. To be true to who you are, unashamedly.

I hope you choose to be mindful of your counterparts, too. Determine whether those surrounding you are the right support structures for the house you are currently constructing. Never let the external force you to travel down roads you know are not meant for you.

Have the courage to stand up for yourself and set boundaries when needed. Quit saying yes to dates, parties, and outings you have no interest in attending. Start loving yourself and supporting your personal wellness journey. See this chapter in your life as instrumental in bringing you one step closer to where you want to be.

Remember that the *hardest* part is often just getting started—and having the discipline to keep at it, even on days when it is pouring rain and you told yourself you would get to the gym before work. On the days when you lack the desire to cook a new recipe for dinner and heating up a frozen entrée sounds much more appealing. On ones when waking up before the sun rises feels like the zombie apocalypse. Know that these moments are where you get to know yourself most intimately, and that they are also the moments that characterize your growth.

Since you cannot be built overnight, please choose to embrace the process, show love, and stay committed to your standards. Wholeheartedly believe that the person you are becoming is worth fighting for. That she is bold, and that although she may be weathered by the pain, she will be never broken by it. *A masterpiece.*

NON-NEGOTIABLES

As you begin your self-assembly, I hope you get to know your values well.

- What do you stand for?
- What are you willing to go to all lengths to prove?
- What do you live by every single day and expect your inner circle to value, too?

Living a purposeful life is only attainable when you lead with value-driven thinking. Whether it is loyalty, honesty, reliability, or positivity, discerning your beliefs, *and living them out*, is crucial to sustained success. These core principles serve as the basis for your decision-making and identity building. **They are fundamental in your growth, and they need to be prioritized.**

Also, having these specific values in mind helps you understand your non-negotiables—the must-haves in your life that are not open to discussion. These tenets are irreplaceable to you, so if you value honesty, a non-negotiable for you may be never lying to a colleague or a friend because you would never want another person to lie to you. Or it could be avoiding college loans so that you can travel the world after graduation since you value learning about new cultures.

Whatever it is, defining your values permits you to act with intention. It permits you to get comfortable with who you are because you are fully aware of what you stand for.

The thought of completing this task may sound monumental, especially when you have never done this before, but please keep telling yourself that taking this jump will lead you closer to uncovering the potential buried inside of you.

ICE

You may think you are the ultimate ice queen—stealthy, intriguing, enigmatic, and cold—but I hope you know that your snowstorms and blustery winds are all a façade.

That your cold, bitter heart, full of anger, sorrow, and despair, is not a direct reflection of your personality, but a direct reflection of your desire to feel safe. Human beings are habituated to return to safety—not to push themselves past their limits.

The years and years of pain, heartache, and fear you lived with have turned you into someone you are not. *Note that they have not defined you once and for all, though.* They have just taken that little girl who loved basking in the sunshine with a fiery glow in her heart and iced her over. These experiences caused you to feel as if staying frozen in place was the only way to defend yourself against the brutality imposed upon your unguarded heart.

The thing is, though, living in an igloo cannot compare to living in a loving home. Thus, it is time to chip down your icicles and dismantle the spell you have been cast under by taking the steps necessary to change temperatures.

Please move above the freezing point and defrost.

Burn away the snowdrifts that uncontrollably mounted up and step into a world of growth, forgiveness, and change. A universe in which you can define yourself on your own terms—not by the terms ascribed *to* you. One that is willing to love you just the way you are. Know that you are beyond capable of assembling a home within your body that feels just as secure as your igloo once felt.

TICKING CLOCKS

I t is never too late to turn things around.

You are never too far along whatever avenue you are headed down to change courses because **you** are at the helm of your own ship. The amount of water you let drag you down into the vast ocean is solely dependent on your personal threshold.

It is contingent upon your ability to say no in a world where saying no is seen as being selfish, mean, rude, unkind, and unhelpful. On your ability to reclaim your inner voice and accept the consequences implicit in deviating from the norms.

Your clock will keep ticking, and the ticks will keep passing you by the longer and longer you continue debating and evade doing.

SPEECH

I challenge you to begin talking to yourself like you are already your highest self. Talk to yourself like this phase of growth has already ended, and you will find that the more you start acting like your highest self, the closer she comes to being alive.

Tell yourself that until you release the woman you know you truly are, you will never reap the benefits of her wisdom.

That you must live in her skin, love her, and exemplify her until you are fully her.

RESERVES

I f you are always "too tired" to live, how do you expect to maximize your time on earth?

If you constantly stay up later than you should—and you know you shouldn't—*how do you expect to show up for yourself in the morning?*

How can you perform when you are groggy, cranky, and droopy-eyed, hitting snooze for the fourth consecutive ring?

When you are miserable and sleep-deprived, dreading another day of your monotonous routine, painful commute, and boring home life?

It is impossible to consistently function at your highest level without rest. If you are planning to take your wellness journey seriously, you must move sleep from insignificant to priority. You also need to learn the importance of sacrifice, because you will need to sacrifice in order to modify your lifestyle (and your sleeping patterns).

Know that waiting for you on the other side of this shift is a world you have yet to tap into. One where you are not aimlessly scrolling through your social media feed at 1:30 AM, comparing your body to the *"perfect"* girls flooding your screen. Where you wake up feeling grateful to meet another day, execute your goals, and work towards personal and professional success. One where you form meaningful friendships, connect with mentors and professors, and drive yourself to the beach and walk your dog without feeling like you are on empty.

You only get one shot to make your life a high-quality and memorable one. Do not waste it slogging around *"too tired"* to do anything.

BEES TO BLESSINGS

As you begin your self-assembly, notice how many people walk out of your life, disgusted with the fact that you would put yourself above them. Notice how your family members resist the tasks you tell them you can no longer partake in because you have boundaries. And notice that those who were once closest to you no longer understand your motives. That they do not like you as much as the quiet, passive, timid girl you used to be.

I call these people bees.

Know that these bees become irrelevant the further you progress in your assemblage. They sting like wasps at first because their opinions and presence meant everything to you at one point. As you encounter other creatures along your growth journey, though, these bees lose their significance. As you evolve, you meet fascinating, like-minded souls who compliment you. They infiltrate your inner circle because they endorse your values, dreams, and visions. **They also do not sting.**

In this process, you will notice how far outside of your comfort zone you roam, and instead of second-guessing your decisions, you will double down. The components of you that matter most will become most pronounced. The beehive explosion that erupted when you initiated change will remain just that: a temporary outburst. A single moment that removed those who were unaligned with who you were becoming. A blessing in disguise.

An omen disguised as a collapse.

LEAP

I know that you are trying to protect yourself from feeling hurt by refusing to open your heart to the love of a lifetime. To shield yourself from getting let down by refusing to expect positive treatment from anyone. By accepting abuse, screaming matches, and declined calls as random acts instead of as indications of a behavioral pattern—as major red flags that need to be run from as quickly as possible.

I know that you are trying to defend yourself from critics by becoming your own worst critic first. By devouring your confidence so that no one else can surprise you. To safeguard yourself against disappointment by self-sabotaging any efforts you take to advance personally, intellectually, or professionally.

Understand that until you let go of the fear keeping you waiting in life's waiting room—a port where the ships come and go, but you refuse to embark on your voyage—you will never experience elevation. You will never lay yourself bare and heal the wounds preventing you from awakening the most authentic version of yourself.

Please permit yourself to relinquish factors far beyond your control. Push any resistance or hesitation right out the front door, too, because these feelings do not belong in your home, and *they never will*. Keep a positive headspace. Stop ruining your chances of making yourself happy by crippling your self-esteem and numbing your pain. Finally, remember that happiness is not a final destination, but an expedition you willingly choose to take part in every day.

Please dismount. Leap.

What if it turns out better than you could have ever imagined?

ASSET

Would you spend three hundred dollars on the wrong size designer shoes? How about on tickets to your least favorite singer's concert? On a salmon entrée at a restaurant downtown even though you are deathly allergic to fish? I am going to go out on a limb and say that your answer to these questions would be *"no."*

So why, then, do you continue spending your time on people, places, and things that are not right for you whatsoever?

On *"friends"* that intentionally bring you down, pick apart your outfits, and make you feel awful about yourself—all because they are so insecure and jealous themselves that they cannot accept your happiness.

On commuting to work two hours each way just to say that you have a fancy job in a luxurious city, although you cannot afford to spend time with loved ones.

How about on forty-five-minute episodes of your favorite show that cause you to examine your worth and attractiveness?

Please understand that your time equals your dollar. That the decisions you make surrounding your time allocation reflect themselves as life satisfaction or as total exhaustion.

As such, you must be just as calculated with where you invest your time as you would with where you invest your money. How much time you save for yourself, for the things, people, and places that matter most, is a direct gauge of your success.

Instead of burning yourself out by accruing heaps of debt in wasted time, remember that your time is your greatest asset and that it needs to consistently be treated as such.

LOCKED DOORS

There is so much strength in knowing that you want to enact change in your life. No matter how big or small, I hope you are proud of yourself for recognizing there are aspects of your reality that do not align with where you are headed.

The first step in assembling your ideal self is pinpointing areas you are willing to work on. You need to know your starting line in order to orchestrate a plan. It is only from this place that you can construct a home you genuinely enjoy living in. Getting honest on this level is not easy, but it is undeniably worth it because you prove to yourself that you are willing to do the work. That you want what you have identified so badly that nothing can stand between you and it. That you are aware of the long hours you will spend working towards your dreams, and that you opt to see them as unforgettable instances.

Reaching your goals does not happen when you sit still. It happens when you mobilize and strategize. Knowing that you want to transform is the first *"knowing"* you need to know that you are worth it. That you are beautiful just as you are now, and that the renovations you intend to make will only augment this fact—*not spawn it into existence*. That you are brilliant enough to do whatever you set your mind to, and that implementing self-education, exercise, and reading into your life will enhance your soul.

On days when you fail to see the needle moving, remember why you started. Recall the courage it took to get real with your emotions, set yourself on the right path, and clarify your vision. Reminisce on the resistance you overcame to find keys that allowed you to unlock locked doors.

NO PEACE, NO POWER

Remind yourself that forces beyond your control do not control you. They may make you feel stuck, but it is ultimately your *reaction* to these forces that controls you.

Your reaction is the key to your freedom.

As such, you must learn to accept that with which you have zero say. The family member that irritates you. The parking ticket you got for running two minutes over at your nail appointment. January's latest snowstorm that inconveniently ruined any shot you had at attending your first date on Saturday night. The friend of an old friend who spread rumors about you without knowing you. These circumstances are unfortunate, but in order to evolve, you must bolster your mental resilience.

You must figure out your pillars and allow them to thrive within you. You must shut out the chatter and know that you are more than capable of rewiring your inner narrative and your perceptions. You have to liberate yourself from the rule of volatility.

You must do all of these things because being around dead weight—the weight of the uncontrollable—not only perpetuates your worries about life, but it also drives you straight into the ground. Without peace, there is no power, and without power, life swoops you away.

UNCOVERING

Until you give yourself power, and encourage yourself to grow and live and smile and dance in the rain, nobody else can help you accomplish your feats. No matter how hard they try, or *"care,"* or *"should be supporting you better,"* they cannot do much if you are not acting as your own biggest cheerleader first.

The tools you need to evolve already exist within you. They may be dusted over, buried under a rug of hate, despair, and sadness, but they are patiently waiting for you to extract them.

DETERMINATION

Maybe it is all about being content with your journey regardless of the obstacles and roadblocks you will inevitably tackle. Maybe it is about having faith in your ability to bring about the revelations that keep you up at night.

Whatever speaks to you, know that there will be more satisfaction found in *getting* to that place than there will ever be in *standing still*. Also know that as you refine yourself, set your priorities, and lead in a new cadence, some people may never clap for you. They will turn their backs, speak poorly about your character, and roll their eyes.

It does not matter.

Those people do not get to live in your skin every single day. They do not know what it feels like to be brave and take bold jumps, either. You need to accept that the mental, physical, or emotional pain they are dealing with has nothing to do with you. You cannot let the lack of attention or acceptance you receive from others derail your plans.

Choose to channel your determination into awakening the woman within you because with yourself, you can conquer any disturbance.

MY ENEMY

The greatest competition you will face as you architect this riveting home within yourself *is* yourself.

It is the resistance pumping through your veins—unrelenting in pressure and increasingly more destructive in nature. It is your harmful standards, pessimistic mindset, and lack of discipline. It is the degrading thoughts you permit into your consciousness. And it is failing to remember that *you* are ultimately in control of your brain. That whatever you let permeate between the subconscious and conscious stays. It is that being your own personal gatekeeper, and filtering out thoughts that discourage progress, is the only way to block them before they brew. It is the passes you keep giving yourself and it is the picking yourself apart.

Stop being your own worst enemy.

PLAYING CARDS

Remind yourself that life has *not* stacked the cards against you, contrary to what your mind may persuade you to believe.

The only way you keep in this pattern of thinking is by resisting thoughts that do not follow the guidelines you have allowed yourself to live by all these years.

Reorient your mindset, deal yourself a new hand, and see what happens.

QUIET

As you initiate evolution, you will have to become skilled at quieting the voice in your head. The one that avoids uncharted territory just like a boat that deliberately rows backward into rough seas after overcoming tidal waves and escaping to calmer waters.

Know that when you enact positive change, no matter how highly sought out that change may be, you may feel uncomfortable *living* in that change until you familiarize yourself with it. During this period of discomfort, your stress may increase to the point where you struggle to actually feel happy about your achievements.

This is because you worked so hard to accomplish your goals that now that you have them in the palm of your hand, you cannot fathom losing them.

Now that you have gotten in shape, you wonder what will happen if you eat a cupcake or skip a workout—thereby reversing all the progress you made.

Now that you are doing your dream job, you struggle with imposter syndrome.

Your subconscious wiggles its way under your skin right when the sun starts shining. It makes you feel like the second one battle is conquered, you are already onto the next worry with no time to fully appreciate your win.

I hope you realize that learning to tame this instinctual reaction—to cease resisting unfamiliarity—will be imperative in your continued success.

SILVER LINING

B e gentle with yourself on the days you struggle to put one foot in front of the other. On the days when darkness pervades your view, and you cannot seem to find the tenacity to go any further. On ones when teardrops roll down your face like an endless stream, and you label yourself as pathetic. These days will come because they *always* do.

Choose not to beat yourself up on these days because you have survived so many battles that you swore were going to be the end of you. Moments that made you question whether you had what it took to lift yourself out of the rubble. Every single difficult day, ugly cry, necessary scream, and brutal heartbreak you have faced, you have made it out on the other side.

Your life is not meant to be easy, either, **because it is in the struggle where you get to know how strong you truly are.**

To appreciate the highs, you must know what it means to face problems head-on—and to defeat them. You must understand your ability to confront challenges, and you must understand that this ability helps you regain ownership of the woman hiding inside you.

BURN

Maybe the scariest thing you can do is allow your untapped potential to remain stagnant within you. To marinate within your heart, mind, and soul, but to never act on it. To never take the strides needed to transform the life you have now into one that reflects your deepest desires.

Allowing that potential to whirl around inside of you, but never bringing it to the light of day, is the equivalent of blowing out a candle before ever giving it the chance to burn.

Know that with the finite amount of time you have on earth, *not* chasing your dreams is a costly mistake. Refusing to recapture your inner voice only brings you closer to shutting down your potential for good. Enabling a breeding ground for unrealistic expectations, negative self-image, low self-esteem, lingering trauma, and unfounded, fear-based thinking does, too.

DO IT FOR YOU

Work in silence. Make a commitment to yourself in silence. There is no need to announce the changes you intend to make within yourself amongst a crowd, no matter how compelled you may feel to do so.

Your life is meant to be lived by you and for you only. While gaining approval for your transformation may feel comforting in the moment, you are doing yourself more harm than good because you are relying on others to give you the green light to live the life of your dreams. *What happens when they change their minds and no longer support you?* Does this mean that you now need to give up on yourself since they did, too?

The authorization you give yourself to work on yourself does not need to commence at the convenience of another person's timeline.

Because of this fact, I hope you show up for yourself every single day until you have assembled your disjointed components into something extraordinary. I hope you make light of your current situation instead of allowing it to make a *mess* out of you. Lastly, I hope you work hard without needing another human to clap for you because people only cheer when it is appropriate for them.

ENVIRONMENT

I hope that today, you give yourself permission to organize your space. To declutter your overflowing drawers, dust off your countertops, and straighten up your living room cabinets. To implement a filing system for your personal and professional assets, pick your dirty clothes up off the hardwood floor, and wash your pillowcases and sheets so they are clean, soft, and silky.

Your environment—the organization of your environment—is a direct reflection of the legitimacy of your wellness journey. The tidier your space, the more room exists for you to grow into it. The cleaner your surfaces, the brighter the sunshine can glisten off the top of them and onto your radiant face.

Choose to surround yourself with items and photos that encourage you to move forward—not ones that dredge up a troubled past by highlighting failed relationships, missed chances, broken promises, and horrible vacations. Evaluate why you cling onto clutter, too. Ask yourself if this mess is a projection of your inner turmoil, and whether you are using this very chaos to stay in your comfort zone. In a place you have become so tightly attached to that working towards any mile marker sends you running back for security, safety, and normalcy.

I hope you release what no longer serves you and eliminate clutter because these practices plant the seed for a life of prosperity.

LOVER

I f you are still on the fence about making a necessary shift within yourself, and cannot seem to find your why, think about this statement: **how can you expect to love another—to gain that incredibly deep connection you desire—if you are not able to love yourself?**

How can you expect to give yourself to another if you are not able to heal your own wounds? How can you expect another to give themselves to you if *they* are unsure who you truly are, because *you* are unsure who you truly are, too?

Know that the key to a long-lasting, magnetic relationship is not pouring your broken heart and fragile soul into another human being. It is also not finding *"the one"* by mindlessly scrolling through dating apps until you stumble across your perfect match.

The key is pouring your own cup *first*. It is being so comfortable in your own skin that you are ready to love another with the same energy you have been pouring into yourself all along. It is feeling complete within your body and not hiding from your insecurities by using a partner to cover up the inner problems you are too scared to face alone.

This is the key because no one else can love you for you who truly are—flaws and all—until you understand who you truly are *first*. No one else can compensate for your lack of self-love with flowers, chocolates, sweet messages, and reassuring displays of affection, either.

With this in mind, you must now decide if you are willing to give up a chance at experiencing the love of a lifetime because you are not courageous enough to self-assemble.

HER

No matter what you are going through, you need to stay strong. You need to stay strong for yourself. For the world, because the world needs you, too. *And I need you. We need you.*

We need your brilliance, your highest self, your creativity, your smile, and your genius. We need the warrior who has been locked in her cage for far too long.

Know that you need to stay strong because your strength will empower those around you. Your strength will be the light that carries your community members, friends, and loved ones out of the darkness. You need to stay strong for yourself as well, because when you are on the other side, your newfound resiliency will prove how integral your struggles were in your success.

Remember that you are a force who is not willing to take no for an answer. Who will not lie down when the odds are against her, sparkles in the face of adversity, and does not accept the terms prescribed to her in life as a declaration of fate.

It is the challenges that bring you closest to who you really are. **To her.**

OPINIONS

I t is far too easy to let the opinions of others set the tone for your wellness journey. **It is far too easy to let them govern your life altogether.**

The concerned parents who push you towards a lifestyle they always envisioned you enjoying base their pleas on idealized images lodged deep within their minds. They cannot fathom telling you to run after what it is you *actually* need because they are unable to drop the fantasy they designed in their heads years before you were conceived.

The friends who dull your enthusiasm about your new spin certification do so because they cannot live to see you happy, fit, and healthy.

Allowing these individuals to reorient your picture of success—to define the terms for which a *"happy life"* is experienced—is to let go of yourself entirely. You must be daring enough to stand tall and let the world know that you have what it takes to author your own story. That tyranny, commonplace rules, and stereotypical ways of being must take a back seat because you do not answer to those who have never walked in your shoes.

Hold your head high because you already know that you can forge a satisfactory route. A route that ultimately helps you assemble regardless of outside chatter.

THE WEEKENDER

If you find yourself living for the weekend, you need to act.

You need to stop lying to yourself by thinking that it is normal to live every weekday in a hurry, daydreaming about how much better life will be on Friday night when you order sushi takeout and get to sleep in. **Living this way is not healthy for you.**

It not only makes you more resentful of the things in your life, but it also wrecks your morale. It eats away at your subconscious and eliminates the beauty woven through the small moments. It causes you to miss the important social interactions linked with living in the *now* because you live solely in a world of daydreams. In a world where all that matters is the future—which is not real.

If this resonates with you, you owe it to yourself to inspect what is making you so unhappy. Once you have uncovered that component, *get rid of it*. Improve upon the systems you have in place so that you can enjoy each day equally. So that you can take time slowly and feel fulfilled whether it is Tuesday morning at your desk or Saturday night at dinner with friends.

ALERT

Consider the signs that push you to release any hesitation you have towards change. Your life will give you these signs, you just need to be attentive enough to catch them. It could be a young girl playing in the park, carefree and full of happiness—reminding you that it is really not that deep. Or a flight attendant who has the same name as your grandfather—reminding you that you should keep in touch more frequently.

In a less curious life, you may forgo these signs as everyday interactions, but when you are looking for meaning, you will find it. You just need to be observant and thoughtful enough to analyze random occurrences that are really not that random at all. They are not random because they push you to expand your knowledge base and submit to the flow of your life.

Now that it is time to let the signs in, you can find out exactly what you have been missing. You can live in the now and stay alert.

ADJUSTING

One of the most important parts of this step in your growth project is modifying your headspace from one that *resists* growth to one that *embraces* meaning and purpose.

Know that as you partake in this transition, you experience the joy of knowing your disturbances are behind you. You feel the satisfaction interlaced with beating the beast. You can remove uninvited guests from your command center and disassociate from your subconscious.

You can ultimately realize that what once brought you to your knees now gives you the strength to fight back harder.

SURVEYING

If you were surveying the land you intended to build your home on, would you take a surface-level assessment and then buy? Would you turn a blind eye to muddy swamps and caving patches since you are so eager to get a move on production?

Any real estate agent or contractor would tell you that this is the quickest way to expend your energy—your time—on a project that you have yet to vet out.

The same goes for your self-assembly.

Remember that your body is your home's construction site. A place of excitement, untapped potential, and enduring dreams. Between your strong bones, warm heart, and thick skin lie all the battles you have won—and all the ones you courageously fight each day. The scars, stories, and sensations that bring back into focus just how human you are. Your home is where you will live your whole life, too. The chambers of your mind keep you grounded. Your legs carry you, step by step, towards success.

Without a durable foundation and a genuine authorization to conduct your plans, know that you will wind up just like that home buyer I mentioned earlier—broke and discouraged.

Please choose to dig deep beneath the surface. Build yourself up. Architect your ideal reality. Before you fully give yourself to another, commit yourself to a career, or travel in the wrong direction out of spite, make it a point to excavate what is not meant for you.

Give yourself permission to create the home within yourself that you have always yearned for.

LENDING A HAND

F air warning that in your assembly, you may be tempted to take shortcuts. To find quicker ways to cross off your checklist and walk through the end of the tunnel.

Instead of concentrating on getting to the place you desire to be, I challenge you to take each phase as a chance for self-reflection. As an opportunity to ensure your goals are aligned with your truest self.

I also hope you clearly communicate your intentions to refurbish yourself with the women you love most. Fellow women cannot stand with you if they do not know where you stand in the first place. Do not be afraid to ask for help as you launch this undertaking—you never know which doors can open for you until you wedge your foot in and accept support.

You have not come this far to *only* come this far. You are ready to reflect upon the things that have hurt you, set attainable principles, and work to better your reality. As such, you cannot fear fellow women who are willing to lend a hand. In its place, you should fear not trying at all.

You should fear failing to actualize the woman you truly are.

INHALE, EXHALE

As much as planning is important—because it is important—it is just as important to take life one day at a time. To take a second to breathe. **Inhale and exhale.**

This journey can become all-consuming at times. It alters your normal and changes your perspectives about life, love, partnerships, and, most importantly, yourself. It improves, embodies, and defines you at such a rapid pace.

Because of these facts, you need to step back and appreciate your path while you are still on it.

Inhale and exhale.

THE GOALS

I hope you choose to set personal goals that are challenging but thrilling. Ones that line up with your principles, feel realistic and attainable, and do not conflict with your identity.

I hope you choose to set big goals for yourself, too. For example, instead of giving yourself ten years to complete a task, give yourself two years. Maybe you will fall short, but I can assure you that you will be much farther ahead in those two years than you would be if you gave yourself eight additional years to accomplish the *same* mission.

I hope you pinpoint mile markers along the way that mirror your construction plans as well. Think of steps you can take to ensure the conflicts you are facing today are not the same ones you are facing six months from now because starting any effort is hard, but channeling the crux of your existence is a whole different ball game.

Acting with dedication and persistence, and being disciplined enough to stay true to systems that awaken your inner voice, is essential to sustained triumph.

Your struggles are bringing you to a place unlike any you have known before.

RECORD

As you embark on this voyage of loving yourself again, of feeling at home in your skin, I hope you document your progress. You do not need to do this every single day, though. Maybe do so when you notice a profound shift within yourself, or when you feel most discouraged.

I hope you keep a journal to track your growth and note what has specifically stirred within you. Write down any significant patterns or lessons you have acquired in this process. I hope you also detail why you are feeling scared, upset, or angry with your progress. And that you take pictures and save them in an album on your camera roll.

These are all instrumental in celebrating the steps you are taking because results are not quick or apparent. Results happen through small moments of acceleration. If you do not clap for yourself in these instances, you will discount them as unimportant, and doing so totally debilitates your self-esteem and resolve.

Most of all, by keeping an eye on your progress, you take back control over your life. You can clearly tell the changes in your outlook, in the way you speak about yourself, and in the way you master obstacles you thought you would never tame.

HOME

POV: that feeling when you are returning from an extended vacation, and although you know you will miss the Caribbean breeze and sandy shores, part of you yearns for your bed.

For that cozy spot in your room where the light shines in and perfectly illuminates the pages of your favorite novel. For that shower, THE shower, which washes away your worries, leaving you refreshed, clean, and wholesome again. For that drive down those all-too-familiar back roads singing to your favorite songs and grabbing a cup of coffee along the way. For that moment you open the door to your house, and it looks just the way you left it… but changed.

Same couch, same utensils, same rug, same shoe rack, but nonetheless, different. Lived. Experienced. Altered. It is as if those eight days away shifted your understanding of what it means to be home. What the furniture, paint, and doors look like now has a new meaning. *Was that chair always such a rosy red? Did the carpet always feel so fuzzy between your toes?*

Remember that the peace that comes with knowing that you have your own space, on your own time, to utilize whichever way you like, is simply precious. A private enclave guarded against outside pressures, stigmas, and stereotypes. A place to breathe and let loose, get comfortable, and exist. It is also a place you do not value enough until you wander off track for a while. It is a destination you are so accustomed to that you hardly appreciate its significance.

It is your home.

It is truly what you make of it, how you perceive it, and the lengths you are willing to go to preserve it that counts. Your home will always be there, even if it changes every so often. Know that although you are evolving, you will always find solace at home.

PART 2
PRIMING

ENACTING

Laying the foundation for a life you can be proud of starts and ends with your perspective. It starts and ends with the way you approach the present moment. With your ability to eradicate negative thoughts, practice mindfulness, and enhance your inner narrative.

Thus, I hope you scrap any places, people, or situations that bring you down. They cannot hold weight in your life because you will not let negators dictate your future. Life is far too short to entertain individuals who disrupt your peace.

Stop putting on a front and be candid instead. Have the courage to admit your faults and the desire to start new again. Get honest about when you have stumbled in the past and WHY. *Why did you break down? Why did you act out of character?* Was it because you did not know who you really were, and therefore could not act in accordance with your highest self?

Whatever the answer may be, know that a fresh slate is in closer proximity than you could ever imagine. You owe it to yourself to untiringly chase your dreams and walk with resolve every single day. Achieving your ideals is only possible when you take action to build from the ground up and end pain avoidance.

It is only attainable when you take the time to set a foundation that can serve as the basis for an empowered, sturdy home within yourself.

LOAD-BEARING

The formal definition of a foundation is *"the lowest load-bearing part of a building, typically below ground level"* (Oxford Languages). Think of this as your base, as the underpinning that regulates how powerful of a structure you can assemble.

Irrespective of the plans and authorization you gave yourself in the first section, if you do not take time to work through the underlying tenets of your life, you will continue to falter. With this in mind, I hope you:

- Delve into the narratives entrenched in your subconscious.

- Learn from past mistakes and treat them as opportunities for advancement.

- Get brutally honest about which of your disorganized components no longer benefit you. *Think of your habits, relationships, and responsibilities.*

- Lay the groundwork for a principled, value-driven reality.

- Refuse to discount the struggles you have endured.

- Wholeheartedly and fearlessly believe in yourself.

- **Never give up on the woman you are becoming.**

Know that when you stand for nothing, you are susceptible to follow the lead of others instead of following the lead of your own pack. You absolutely do not need to walk down someone else's path, so please stop borrowing someone else's foundation, standards, or identity as a substitute for building your own. This practice only prevents you from genuine realization and bliss.

Without a foundation you are incapable of assembling. *Of becoming.*

WATERFALL

Picture yourself hiking up the side of a waterfall for the first time. Envision the beauty you witness from your car ride to the base of the hike: the cascading water, luscious trees, and outstanding terrain. It all seems so exciting, new, and fresh... stunning. Once you get to the starting point, your shoes are strapped, your helmet is on, and you are ready to go. **You look up.**

Suddenly, you hesitate.

Am I really cut out for this? Is this safe? Am I going to make it to the top, or am I going to humiliate myself in front of all these people?

Your thoughts start to swarm because you are trying to defend yourself from expanding beyond your limitations. Your body does not take kindly to practices that endanger your safety bubble. The world you have shielded yourself into, reinforced with experience, and maintained out of fear does not want to evolve.

The thing is, though, you have perpetuated these constraints for far too long. It is time to face the things that scare you the most. It is time to do so in a way that honors your truest self while simultaneously encouraging you to grow.

In this practice, you learn that the climb to the top of your waterfall is where you learn the most about yourself. You learn that creating the foundation for your own home is a process that teaches you about what you *need* in your life. You realize that reasoning with yourself when you are overwhelmed is a superpower. You discover that your demeanor must reflect your truest desires and align with your direction.

Please do not shy away from the climb of a lifetime. The view at the summit will be worth the setbacks you endure during your climbing expedition.

DAY ONE

I n case you forgot, no one's day four hundred is going to resemble your day one. It is just not possible.

There are so many mistakes to make, wins to celebrate, and details to iron out as you progress towards actualizing your objectives. This is natural—*this is what is supposed to happen*. You are not supposed to start off winning at everything and feeling light and breezy. And if that is how you feel right now, know that your dreams are not daunting enough.

You are not challenging yourself enough because if you consistently feel like you have it all together, like you are the smartest, the richest, the hardest working in the room, then you are in the wrong room.

You are obliged to escape that room and put yourself into a space where you feel the need to change and overcome.

It is through this practice that you naturally learn the most, so cease comparing where you are today to anyone else's position in life. They were where you are right now at one point, but the difference between them and you is that they tamed the noise and kept moving forward *despite* it.

Now, you must do the same.

NAVIGATE

You ou were born to become the highest version of yourself. You just never reached the point of needing to actualize that very being until now, but today, **you are ready**.

In order to release the trauma lying within your bones, your healing is now necessary. Your misfortunes, mistakes, and mishaps must be forgiven so that you can excel. Your habits must be corrected so that you can officially quash your self-sabotaging behaviors. Your life stories need to be journaled about so that you do not forget all the terrifying and enlightening experiences that brought you to the present.

Think of this as your life's agenda, as a natural process you did not know you were destined to embark upon until now.

Remember that the purpose of going through tough times is not to retreat to your starting point: it is to acquire the courage, elasticity, and confidence to transcend your *prior* circumstance. To view pain as a pressure inducer that does not squish the life out of you, but as one that crafts you into the diamond you have always been.

It is all about jumping into the unknown and trusting that you will find a way to navigate through.

HEADSPACE

P lease understand that factors beyond your control cannot serve as excuses for your *inability* to revise your headspace.

They are undeniably obstacles that must be worked through, and they *will be* worked through because you are more than capable of doing the work. You are more than capable of catching yourself whenever you label the uncontrollable aspects of your world as restraints.

As long as you do not let them become restraints, they will never be ones.

COMPASS POINT

Your direction is far more important than your speed.

Know that although you may move at a slow pace, *it is okay*. Slow is okay because slowness makes room for acceleration. It enables moments where your ship pushes far faster than usual. This rush of momentum surprises you at first, but then you recognize that in order to experience bursts of action, you inherently *need* sluggishness. A sense of calmness and steadiness allows for the opposite—quick, swift, tactical—to enter center stage.

Slowness and speed are counterbalancing forces of nature.

While your boat may act less like a speedboat and more like a raft at times, I hope you learn to be okay because it is in the spurts of full acceleration that you undoubtedly make incremental climbs. As your gears shift, your limits swell, too. Your sense of normalcy inflates beyond the shoreline where you set off into the ocean and ventured into this assemblage.

All that matters right now is that you are moving with a sturdy foundation in place. The momentum, speed, and acceleration you seek will come when you need it most. Hold on tight and never give up on yourself.

Your commitment and direction take precedence above all else.

AWARE

You will find that self-awareness is imperative in unraveling the blueprint that outlines the home you are constructing within yourself.

It reveals the rituals, directions, objectives, emotions, relationships, and outlooks that elevate your conscious. The ones that take you from where you are now to where you need to be. To new heights far beyond the self-imposed boundaries you have been dwelling between. Beyond your bubble.

Understand that until you become self-aware, you will never be able to access your blueprint. This is destructive because having a home within yourself is not just about having a place to rest at day's end, or an abode of comfort, refuge, and peace. It is having a **residence** that grounds and reinforces growth.

I encourage you to step back and ask yourself what work needs to be done in order for you to gain this deep sense of awareness. *Where can you renovate? Which components of yourself can be woven into the truest version of yourself?*

Mapping out your strategy for building this home may sound like a formidable task, but by working through the tough moments, you awaken the woman hiding underneath the baggage you have carried around for far too long.

SECRET ADMIRER

I admire you.

I admire your ability to keep your composure when others try everything in their arsenal to yank you down. They may loft every weapon at their disposal, but none are strong enough to get inside your mind. To change you into someone you know you are not and knock you off-balance into a retroactive cycle.

I admire the courage you exhibit every time you face an obstacle head-on and refuse to back into your comfort zone. For all the times you have dismantled stereotypes, broken the rules, and invented a route society told you that you could not wander down. I admire your willingness to try new foods, visit unexplored countries, and adopt rituals from foreign cultures. For all the failures you have learned from instead of engaging in negative self-talk. I admire the way you keep your head up high and your crown on straight when surrounded by strangers who chip away at you—the very strangers who do not know, *and could never know*, who you truly are.

I admire your honesty, loyalty, and outlook on life. I admire your work ethic, too, because no matter the situation, you always find new ways to rise. To leave an impression on every single person who crosses your path.

I admire you for everything you stand for.

I wish one day the world would lay down its pride and take a minute to learn how to be just like you. *Thank you for being you.*

CALCULATED RISKS

E ducate yourself on the concept of calculated risks:

"A hazard or chance of failure whose degree of probability has been reckoned or estimated before some undertaking is entered upon" (Oxford Languages).

1. Figuring out what you are getting yourself into prior to taking the leap.

2. Making decisions that are smarter, numbers backed, and well thought out, as opposed to jumping headfirst into a disaster.

In life, know that there are going to be moments where you need to go the riskier route. I do not mean this only in terms of picking stocks and building an investment portfolio. I mean in moving across the country for a job that provides you with higher pay, better hours, and more time to spend with your children. I mean in deciding to cash out on your 401k early to buy your first piece of real estate. I mean in terminating an engagement because you know your partner is not right for you and you have been lying to yourself all this time.

Life is full of choices that amount to the sum of your reality.

When you are faced with a decision that carries weight, choose to get tactical about it. Take it upon yourself to read up and calculate the pros and cons. Come to a conclusion that reflects your values and find the answers written within the opportunity itself.

PLANS

Having no plan equals planning to fail.

Ask yourself if the plan you set in action when you authorized this development journey still represents the crux of your identity. Time inherently changes your perspectives, hopes, and dreams. It can plant the seed for a refined goal or better method, too. This is perfectly normal and okay, but what is not okay is failing to adapt your plan to meet your tempered lens.

Your aim is not to move backward as you assemble, but to set in motion a process that brings you closer to your highest self than you have ever been before. Although this is a hefty task, it is one that you can absolutely accomplish so long as you acclimate to pivots.

No matter how great things are going, I can almost guarantee you that an unexpected expense, jealous friend, vengeful ex, or complete stranger will impede upon your development. **They will not leave a lasting imprint so long as you are grounded in who you are.**

Know that anything you encounter as you reinvent yourself will be survivable with the right plan and the right degree of flexibility.

ENOUGH

I f someone makes you feel like you are not enough for them, I want you to know that there is nothing wrong with you and there is something wrong with them.

There is a reason why they are not satisfied with you, and that has *nothing* to do with you. It has to do with their inability to compromise, their stubbornness and hardheadedness. With the fact that they are so high on their ego that they do not feel any other person in the world would be enough for them.

Bending over backward and trying to force someone to love you only degrades you. It only degrades you because you are going to all lengths humanly possible to be the person someone else needs you to be instead of being the person you need you to be. Instead of realizing that if that person truly loved you, they would encourage you to be yourself, too.

They would never pressure you to shape-shift and fit their needs.

Please stop letting yourself feel like you are not enough for someone else because trust me, all you need to be is enough for *yourself*. Also, remember that you will be okay with or without them because you have been through enough to know that there is nothing in this world that can break you like your own mind. You are wise enough to know that someone else telling you that you are not enough for them simply means that you were not with the right person.

It means you sold yourself short and that you now have an opportunity to start over.

EDUCATE YOURSELF FIRST

I f you really want to evolve, pledge to self-education.

It is not enough to rely on your professors, parents, bosses, or social media feed to teach you important lessons. I encourage you to continuously educate yourself on topics that coincide with your dreams, visions, and goals. Subjects that get you from point A to point B.

Maybe consider subscribing to a newsletter on investment advice for beginners, frequenting nearby art galleries, or enlisting in a freelance writing seminar. Or signing up for courses that refine your transferable skills, improve your chances of landing your dream job, and make you a more competitive candidate in the job market. Reading, listening to podcasts, attending master classes, and having deep conversations with your peers are great ideas as well.

Absorb as much information as possible. Tell yourself that your education is in your own hands. That the energy you invest in teaching yourself will be reflected in your income and growth. Take it upon yourself to be informed. Please do not give others the power of dictating the quality of your knowledge base because knowledge is power, and power is **liberation**.

RESILIENCY

Remember that you own your actions. You own your responses, outlooks, and decisions.

The moment you start believing this, you will notice that sunshine always arrives after rainstorms... and that it sticks around for a long, long while. Once you have battled through enough of these storms, and prioritized your growth, your outlook will permanently shift.

You will grow stronger and more resilient by way of experience. By way of *owning* your experiences.

DELAYED GRATIFICATION

I hope you think of this foundation-setting initiative as an exercise in **delayed gratification**. Put plainly, this practice involves *"the act of resisting an impulse to take an immediately available reward in the hope of obtaining a more-valued reward in the future"* (Oxford Languages).

You are forgoing the temptation of momentary pleasure by remembering why you started. By remembering the indulgences you will experience once your goals are attained. By recalling your values and the necessity implicit in this journey.

By delaying your experience of pleasure, you will also be one step closer to solving your issues because gratification comes once you have worked through the pain nodes obstructing your view. This feeling is more fruitful than you can imagine.

I know you are tired of fighting yourself and being dissatisfied with your day-to-day routine. Soon enough, you will be filled with immense gratification.

INTERLUDE

Remind yourself that you can achieve whatever your context allows you to picture, and that you can make light from darkness. That you can fly through windstorms, overcome setbacks, and shock yourself. That you can learn to appreciate the warmth inherent in actualization and celebrate the vanishing of thoughts that once used to pervade your imagination.

GREENERY

Picture yourself as a houseplant. Cute, green, and prosperous.

You know that taking care of a plant means you must water it based on how much water the particular species needs. You put it in the sunlight or shade depending on the species' needs as well. There is no generic way to take care of a plant because every single plant is *different*. Every single plant is *special* in the way it looks, in its biology, and in its fundamental needs. This is why houseplants come with tags that instruct owners how to keep them alive.

Human beings are just like houseplants. Think of yourself as your own unique houseplant species. As such, you must learn how to tend to your own individualized needs.

How often do you need to exercise, spend time alone, sleep, or go out with friends to feel fulfilled? How much time outdoors, with your partner, in school, or working towards your career targets do you need to feel happy? To feel content with your time allotment?

Maybe you should write out a plant tag for yourself. Ask yourself, if someone were just meeting you for the first time, and you had to give them a how-to guide on how to best take care of you, what would you include?

Know that if you cannot answer these questions, **no one else can treat you the way you *think* you deserve to be treated if you are not entirely direct about *what treatment* you deserve.**

MY BEST FRIEND

If you are going to make yourself a promise, please let it be this one: that you will choose to be your own best friend first. *Unconditionally.*

That you will choose to shower yourself in compliments, see the beauty beneath the pain, and advocate for yourself when nobody else will. That you will understand and treat yourself better than anyone else ever could. And that you will set boundaries instead of guzzling your energy from the very start.

That you will never give up on your passions because you, and only you, can fulfill them. Most of all, that you will walk with courage, perseverance, and calmness in your heart because you know that no matter the result, you will survive.

WHY NOT

Know that there are always going to be a million reasons why you **should not** do something:

1. There are always going to be a million reasons why you should not bother going to the gym—because you are so out of shape and people will stare at you on the treadmill.

2. You will find reasons why you should not spend an hour cooking for yourself and blow your paycheck on take-out meals instead.

3. You will find a way to convince yourself that you should not travel around the world—because the flights are too long, and you do not speak the language in that country, and you will not have any company.

4. Your mind will tell you that you should not say how you feel—because you do not want to lose your best friend, and you do not want to offend her, and you will sound stupid.

5. That you should not walk to school—because there is a chance it may rain today, and you cannot get your hair wet or be inconvenienced.

6. There will be a reason why you should not go to prom—because you do not have a date, and you hate your dress, and you will have nobody to dance with at the end of the night.

7. You will locate a reason for why you should not go away to college—because you cannot leave your siblings at home by themselves, and you are scared of uncharted territory.

8. That you should not publish your book, blog, or channel—because no one will pay attention to it anyways, and it takes too long to grow, and it is too hard to perfect.

Constantly remind yourself that if you accept these reasons as truths, you will never achieve anything in life. **Instead, think of the one reason why you SHOULD.**

OLIVE BRANCH

L ay down your arms. Call off the fighting and terrorizing you have permitted in excess. Stop knowingly causing yourself an immense amount of pain. **End the war inside of yourself.**

You are tearing yourself apart when the only thing you should be doing is building yourself up. The only thing you should be doing right now is watering your seeds and watching your flowers sprout out of the dirt and into the sunlight.

Know that I do not care how discouraged, disappointed, or confused you feel. Or how worthless you think you are, or how incapable you believe you are of doing anything special in this world. Flaming any emotion you have within you only causes the smoke and ashes to blind your sight. It only causes you to continue moving in circles, round, and round, and round.

Please process the things that make you feel anxious, worried, and defensive because until you stop shutting down every feeling your brain exudes, you will never assemble. The concrete waiting to be poured into your foundation will harden. The war will rage on because you fear facing yourself. You cannot understand your truest desires, wishes, and lusts.

Giving yourself permission to confront your feelings breaks the cycle of dancing in circles. If you are going to do one thing before the end of the day, make it this: extend an olive branch to yourself. Heal whatever has been bothering you for far too long.

WHEN YOU KNOW

Your intuition about the present moment should never be ignored. No matter how nervous you are, **do not shut out what your mind is telling you**.

Do not shut out the muffled voice trying to grab the microphone. This very voice that constantly falls back into the shadows knows you. **It knows the real you.** It knows what is best for you. It can feel the queasiness in your stomach as you act out of character. It can sense the tension between you and your significant other as you fight for approval, attention, and love. It can hear the harsh words you say to yourself as you crawl into bed each night—the lies you tell yourself about your potential. It can see the tiredness across your face, the utter exhaustion you feel from trying so hard to fit into the wrong spaces.

Your body is so much smarter than she seems. Please let her speak.

Give her space to show you her worth and that she is always looking out for your best interests. Give her the ability to explain herself. *She wants you to thrive.* Now, you must give yourself the chance to flourish, too, by standing back and letting her get in the driver's seat.

BOUNCE BACK

You can bounce back from anything.

You have been a fighter from an early age—forced to grow up quicker than those around you, encouraged to mentor your peers, and pressed to overcome unimaginable pain.

On the days when you question whether you have what it takes, know that you do because you are yours *first*. With her, you can walk through any storm and come out clean on the other side. Love yourself deeper than another ever could because without that relationship, **you will inhibit yourself from reaching the place you need to be.**

BLAZE

W hen you fully commit yourself to setting the foundation for a prosperous life, I am sure your mind will concoct its own expectations. This is natural, but if one of your expectations is that this is going to be a seamless, fast process, I need you to redraft that narrative in your head. Today. Now.

Growth is one of the most phenomenal undertakings you will ever experience. As much as this is rousing, I need you to know that it will not happen all at once. In fact, it probably will not happen according to whatever schedule you set in place for this chapter of your life, either.

Growth happens in small spurts.

It comes in and out like waves—retreating from the shoreline, and then roaring back full steam ahead, over and over and over again. Some days you may feel like you are moving backward, eternally stuck in a rip current. On others, you will build enough momentum to ignite a wildfire of growth.

You will blaze past opposition.

SYSTEMATIC

Maybe it is less about setting intentions and plans, and more about setting systems and routines that support your goals. You can have all the motivation, discipline, and excitement in the world to:

1. Cross off your to-do list.

2. Work out five days a week.

3. Hang out with friends more often.

4. Spend ten hours a week working on your side hustle.

5. Decrease your screen time.

6. Wake up thirty minutes earlier.

But without a mechanism to keep you consistent, your goals will not see daylight. **If you can set habits that are easier for you to complete than for you to skip, however, you will see much more *optimal* outcomes.**

Maybe you need to challenge yourself to think of systems that ensure your objectives are met. To schedule five hours into your calendar per month to spend on something you have been dreaming about. Maybe you need to assign specific time blocks for this to occur so that your intentions and willpower can amount to diligent actions. You can set reminders so that you do not forget to maintain the systems you have put into place in future months, too.

Now is the time to stay consistent because your goals will not be actualized without doing so.

STUBBORNNESS

B eing overly stubborn will impede on your construction plans.

If you are not coachable or willing to hear about new ways to complete tasks, you are inherently *unable* to make real change in your life. You are so stuck in your ways, so bound to your ego, that you cannot contemplate any other methods or practices (even those that may be more efficient or rewarding than the ones you are acclimated to now).

Understand that the very core of change involves modifying an existing unit. Change itself is defined as *"the act or instance of making or becoming different"* (Oxford Languages). As you can see, if your mind is set on preserving its current procedures, beliefs, and values without ever considering alternative routes, **you cannot expect to self-assemble**.

If you find yourself nodding your head while reading this paragraph, I challenge you to dismantle the root of your obstinate ways.

- Are you threatened by those who disagree with you?
- Are you unwilling to change your opinions because you think you are superior to everyone else?
- Are you so attached to your theories because you constantly felt threatened growing up and needed to assert your dominance to survive?

Know that walking through life with an impenetrable complex decelerates your growth. Your foundation will be muddied by a lack of affinity for newness when you refuse to acquire knowledge about the world and yourself, and apply these findings to your routines.

Force yourself to advance and let go of your stubborn tendencies.

DUSTING OFF COBWEBS

I f you find yourself headed down a futile path, you should stop right in your tracks.

There is no shame in acknowledging that your course of action is flawed. In fact, you are saving yourself so much mental anguish, unhappiness, and disappointment by pulling your identity back into focus and overhauling components as soon as you locate an issue.

Know that staying with your typical, comfortable ways may bring you momentary relief, but that living a dispassionate life in exchange for this relief is not worth it. Feeling dissatisfied and angry at external circumstances for *"forcing you"* to live a life you did not select for yourself is not healthy or amusing.

You are clever and spirited enough to dust the cobwebs off your shelves and restock your soul with avenues that bring you joy, inspiration, and love.

VALIDATION

I f you are searching for:

1. A relationship to bring you happiness.

2. A companion to dispel your insecurities and make you feel whole again.

3. A mentor to present innovative solutions to your business problems.

4. A partner to treasure every inch of you, every single day, and tell you that you are pretty, funny, kind, and the best.

5. A college counselor to tell you exactly how to get into your dream program.

6. A friend to console you in your loneliness, motivate you in your career, and help you see yourself in a new light.

7. A mother or father figure to fill in the gaps missing from your childhood.

I encourage you to halt your search and **start searching within**, because until you give *yourself* all these things you seek in others, you will *never* be able to find them in others. You will never be able to fully support another human being so long as you cannot take care of and love yourself.

Understand that this entire time you have been digging for more and more in others while neglecting to dig into yourself. You have been feeling let down when you are excluded from plans and worrying about what *"they"* are doing behind your back. You have been begging for another person's attention, love, and approval while doing cartwheels to make them stay. And you have been blaming yourself for every misfortune in your life instead of considering the potential that maybe, just maybe, you are a good person. A great person, in fact.

A great person who is wasting all her valuable time and energy looking for validation in others instead of looking for that same validation within herself. Instead of allowing herself to *be* that someone she is so insistent on finding.

Know that she already exists deep within you. Now, it is your duty to quit rummaging for more and to start locating her.

TERMS & CONDITIONS

Happiness will not come once you finish this assemblage. Happiness will not come in a week, three weeks, or six months from now, either, because happiness will never come if you do not make the most of the present moment. If you do not stop waiting for the stars to align, and if you keep putting unfeasible timelines, ultimatums, and expectations around your happiness.

Happiness only comes when you unconditionally decide that you are happy *today*. When you decide that it does not matter if he likes you back. Or if you cannot afford your dream purse or hit your financial markers this month. When you decide that it does not matter if the stock market crashes, or if your new sports car gets dented, or if your flight to Hawaii gets cancelled.

Recognize that there is never going to be a day when your life is so perfect that you can officially be happy, once and for all. **Happiness starts when you choose to be happy irrespective of what goes on around you.**

It starts when you accept your faults. It starts when you find a way to lean into your values—when you appreciate what you DO have instead of harping on what you DO NOT have. When you rejoice for the fact that you are still here, living to see another day.

When your mindset is preventing you from being happy, understand that you will never, ever be able to find joy. Until you fix your headspace, your intentions around happiness will not matter because they will never be realized. Please stop waiting for one moment, for one degree, for one job, for one significant other to make you happy, and elect to be happy without any terms or conditions.

SUNDAY RESETS

Restorative things you can do this Sunday to recharge your energy for the week:

1. Taking care of yourself with some *"me time."* This practice refocuses your mind, releases tension within your body, and refuels your soul. Giving yourself this time also teaches you about what you gravitate towards, about what ignites and defines you.

2. Stretching.

3. Creating a vision board representative of your interests, aesthetic, and vibe, and hanging it up in the hallway of your home.

4. Figuring out how to save more money, whether that be through high-yield savings accounts, new investment approaches, or enhanced budgets.

5. Journaling.

6. Cooking a new meal—one that hits the three major food groups and gives you the nutrients you need to conquer your tasks.

7. Taking a break from staring at screens.

8. Getting fresh air.

9. Enrolling in a webinar to refine your skills or open your mind to potential career fields.

10. Playing the piano.

11. Reading a novel from your local library.

12. Listening to an informational podcast.

13. Pampering yourself with an enhanced skincare routine.

14. Doing yoga or Pilates.

15. Breathing.

Whatever it may be, I challenge you to spend this Sunday on yourself. None of these activities cost money beyond what you already have in your home, so they are all accessible to you. You just need to exploit these resources so that you can take better care of YOU.

RETURN WINDOW

When you go to the store to return a pair of shoes that are a size too big, and the cashier tells you that you have missed the return window, maybe you need to consider this as a sign.

Not as a sign that you are foolish, stupid, and dumb for missing the deadline. Not as a sign that the policy is foolish, stupid, and dumb, either. Maybe you need to consider this as a sign that you are far past your *own* return date. That you can no longer go back and exchange this new space you have created within yourself for the one that used to occupy your body. Maybe this is a symbol that you are growing, that there is no such thing as sizing down anymore.

Know that sizing down is the equivalent of moving backwards.

Right now, however, you are solely focused on moving forwards. On moving bigger and with more compassion, self-understanding, and motivation than ever before.

On the days when it gets tough and you question your direction, I need you to remind yourself that sizing down is not an option. No matter how much fear, confusion, or temptation fills your bones, and no matter how much you want to go back to your self-prescribed *"comfort zone,"* it is not doable.

Putting yourself in reverse—retreating to old habits and toxic relationships—damages your entire assemblage. It harms the outstanding motions you have already taken. So please, allow yourself to accept empty space because it denotes room for evolution.

There is no need to size down to a life you have already surmounted past.

SHEDDING OFF LEAVES

As your leaves change colors in the fall, from green to red, yellow, and brown, you will shed pieces of yourself that are inconsistent with who you truly are. The ones that cannot stand the winter and cannot last in suboptimal temperatures, as well as the ones that spin out of control at the onset of slight hassles, will fade away.

The longer you focus as the wind knocks off your leaves, the sooner you will notice that *no* leaves will be left by the time the wind finally dies down. This is because your core, which includes your bark, stump, and branches, is the only component of you that can survive any climate. **Your body, your mind, and your soul.**

The leaves that adorn you in perfect conditions may be eye-catching, but they do not comprise the whole of who you are because they do not align with your core. They are not *sustainable*.

Choose to remain completely focused on the present and know that the fluff you are shedding off right now was never really part of who you were to begin with.

LIVE YOUR TRUTH

Her kindness can quell an army of soldiers intent on demise.

Her voice can soothe a baby who has not stopped crying all night.

Her ambition to succeed no matter the circumstances prompts crowds of like-minded others to follow in her footsteps.

Her attitude teaches her peers how to live more efficiently and enjoyably.

Her growth is palpable.

Her gaze is gripping.

Her touch is provoking.

Her mind is more powerful than any other aspect of her existence.

She is you.

You are her because she is *in you*. She has always been in you. Whether you have accepted that feat and worked towards embodying her is a whole different story.

She is graceful and generous, and she has feelings. She is not afraid to show the world her true colors and to lead with integrity, self-respect, and love. She despises those who crouch inside the shell of who they truly are instead of allowing their wings to guide them home. And she can help you learn more about yourself than you could ever imagine.

The only thing she asks for—the only thing she demands—is an opportunity to present herself to you.

Your job is to live your truth because doing so gives *her* the oxygen she needs to breathe.

PUZZLE WORK

When you find yourself getting frustrated with your progress, picture yourself as a jigsaw puzzle. There are so many components of you that are individually impressive, exciting, and important. They are the parts of you that sum up to the **whole** of your existence.

If one puzzle piece is out of place, please do not fret. Do not allow yourself to believe that one misalignment defines you because there are thousands of other factors, emotions, and habits that represent you. If one component needs fine-tuning, or to be reset, *so be it*. You can do this—that has already been established.

You are your own boss and no one else is setting these pieces in place for you. While that may be a scary thought, it should actually be a reassuring one because **no one can dictate your identity other than you unless YOU let it happen.**

Understand that it is less about proving to others that your puzzle is fully in place, and more about proving to yourself that regardless of your puzzle's status, you are content. That you accept yourself no matter what and that one part of you does not equal *all* of you. And that although you can remedy a missing piece or two, you will never scrap the entire project because doing so would erase your existence.

You know that you are here on this earth for a reason, and that this reason can only be defined by you.

VISITATION

If you really want to flesh out the fragments of you that deserve closure, you owe it to yourself to revisit the traumas that lurk in your mind at night. And if you need help in this process—professional help, or help from a friend, parent, or lover—I hope you do not feel any shame whatsoever. At the end of the day, you are **human**.

You are meant to feel emotions, reflect on your experiences, and enable them to change you. You are meant to give yourself the chance to work through the thoughts swirling around inside of you, too.

Know that your instinctual responses to stimuli are rooted in the fiber of your being. These responses have been implanted through social conditioning and years of excess trauma.

Also know that you are responsible for your perceptions, so if you are still permitting unpleasant and painful experiences to cloud your vision, you are doing yourself a huge disservice. Holding a grudge, inhibiting recuperation, and not allowing your body to mitigate pain only hurts you. It hurts your morale and your ability to connect with others. It hurts your chances of overcoming the very barriers you wish to overcome—the ones that will allow you to see clearly and gain closure.

Decide to face your pain head-on and radiate light in a world that so readily needs *your* light. **In a world that so readily needs *you*.**

ETCHED

When I think of the core of who I am, I think of you.

How could I not think of you?

You may no longer be with me, but you exist in me still. You have left an irrefutable mark on my heart. Whether it is a scar or a coating of love, I may never know, but I do know your birthday. I know it because it is the security PIN for my bank account. I do know your address because I dropped you off so many times after class, I could never forget it. Your smile is etched into my mind and trust me, it does not go away with time. *I have tried.*

I do know that I loved you with all my heart. And that when I was with you, I never felt dark. Until the light poured its way out of yours, and out of mine, and suddenly, it was nighttime all the time. You may no longer be with me, but you exist in me today. That is a fact that will not ever go away. Know that although I no longer love you, I think of you still. At moments when I question who I am, I remember the lessons you engraved into my mind like a secret pill. The ones about my potential, my worth, and how I am a different kind. You taught me to love myself, to put myself first all the time.

Maybe you regret that now, because I took your advice and used it to escape from you. Your strong tone and your episodes were brutal but without them, I would have never known how strong I truly am. So thank you for the lessons, for molding my core.

I hope you are doing well and have everything you ever wanted, and more.

ESCAPE ROUTE

I f you feel the need to escape from your life, to constantly run away from the present moment, there is something wrong. I urge you to stop telling yourself that this is just how it is.

That it is normal to feel overly anxious, nervous, and fearful about your current circumstances—that it is normal to live in survivalist mode instead of actually *living*. Instead of embracing new experiences and giving yourself the opportunity to evolve, change your mind, learn something, make mistakes, and be a kid. Instead of feeling safe and worry-free.

Living on the edge may seem like all you have ever known. It may also seem like the only viable way to survive, but this approach causes you serious long-term harm. It pushes you to build your walls up so high that another potential partner, friend, or colleague could never get to know you... *the real you*. It causes you to carry so much resentment, paranoia, and distaste within you as well.

Know that the only way to escape the escapist mode is to set the intention that you will create a life you love waking up to each morning. It is on you, and only you, to get yourself from the edge of the mountain to the top of its highest peak. **To escape your lowest self.**

SOLITUDE

Sometimes, disconnection is all you need. **Solitude is all you need.**

Becoming comfortable alone is one of the most rewarding and empowering acts you can partake in. Not only because solitude is a chance for self-reflection and deep rest, but because it is also a place that unearths your *purpose*. It is a place that enables you to thrive in ways you never thought possible.

So take a break from social media, get off your phone, and flee from the endless cycle of comparison, remorse, and doubt. Forget about the stress, the relationship, the trip, and concentrate on you. Dodge activities that drain your energy. Systematize a routine that expands your horizon, fall in love with new hobbies, become enchanted with nature… ultimately, fall in love with **yourself** all over again.

It is in this withdrawal that you acquire a clean slate. You forge a sturdier foundation that fully supports your new lifestyle and priorities. It is here that you regain your inner voice and awaken your soul.

QUESTIONS

You should not question whether you are worthy of someone else's attention.

Whether you are attractive, sexy, or beautiful enough for your partner. Whether you are special enough to gain the love and approval of others. Whether you have the bravery to survive rainstorms and the strength to confront obstacles head-on.

You are more than enough. You are more than enough for the right people, for your partner, loved ones, and closest friends.

You are more than enough for yourself.

ADVICE

L et yourself be content with who you are. Avoid measuring your potential, values, and identity based on the worth *others* assign to you. Learn to cultivate an aura full of kindness and positivity—one that beats within the very core of your soul. A vibe that emanates in every sentence you utter, every breath you exhale, and every step you take.

Know that bettering yourself only means that you are strengthening the dimensions of yourself that bring you closer to who you truly are. That you are acknowledging your weaknesses, combating the noise, and building a secure habitat you can permanently call home.

THE BIG THREE

Your life is largely a byproduct of *who* you were born to, *where* you were born, and *when* you were born, yet **these three factors are completely outside of your control**.

You do not determine who your parents are, how they raise you, what house you grow up in, what generation you live in, and if you are an older or younger sister or brother. You also do not decide whether your parents want to *be* parents, or if you are an orphan, or if you have financial support.

Understand that none of these things reflect your worth and that they are not linked to your potential because none of these things *guarantee* your outcome.

They may mean that you will have to work harder to get good grades, a better education, a higher paying job, and more respect (there is no arguing that). But know that if you put your mind to it, you can achieve it, no matter your situation.

You have it within you.

You may not see it within yourself yet, but I see it within you now. I know that you are ready to end the pattern into which you were born. I know that you have the dedication to attain the impossible. You can rewrite the rulebook, so please do not blame your upbringing for everything that is wrong with you. Please do not play the victim.

One day you will see that your upbringing is one of the most crucial parts of your success story and that it is not your death sentence.

BREAKS

Promise yourself that you will take mental health breaks. That you will not put too much pressure on yourself all at once. That you will educate yourself on burnout and, more importantly, that you will steer clear of it. That you will listen to your natural cues and recognize when you need to retreat, go for a walk, or take fifteen minutes off.

Then actually do those things.

This whole growth journey is hard. It can get tougher and tougher the closer and closer you come to seeing real progress (to feeling fulfilled). If you try to accomplish your goals too abruptly, recognize that you will feel deflated, let down, and uneasy.

As a remedy, I encourage you to rest. *Actually rest.* Disconnect by taking a weekend offline and running around outside like you are a little kid again. Remember what it feels like to have no responsibilities. To feel the wind blowing through your blonde hair and over your freckled face. Breathe. Enjoy the moment. Smile, laugh, cry, scream. Be alive.

Let yourself take a break because doing so brings you closer to your truest self than you were beforehand. You experience magnificent shifts that inch you closer to assembling the home you crave within yourself. You dig out the parts of you that were buried beneath the hustle, the go-getting, and the demanding work.

Do not cause yourself undue harm by being so extreme with yourself.

A GIFT FROM ME TO YOU

If I could give you one gift to cherish for the rest of your life, it would be to see yourself through my eyes. For you to appreciate and love yourself with an unwavering passion and commitment, and for you to hold yourself to the highest regard—*in the same exact way I do*. For you to take care of, defend, and celebrate yourself as deeply as I do.

For you to realize just how special you are.

You hold the weight of the world on your shoulders, and you find a way to make it look effortless. You do not complain, cower down, or run, but rather, you prevail. You never stop fighting for what you believe in. You never fail to put a smile on a stranger's face, either. You are the epitome of all that is good in this chaotic world.

You are pure and bold.

More than ever, I wish you could see yourself through my eyes because only then would you understand how astounding you truly are.

REPAIR

Healing is how you return home. It is how you go back home to your *truest* self.

Overcoming the incessant thoughts, guilt, and sadness, and gaining clarity, is **priceless**. Letting yourself have peace of mind is priceless. Forgiving yourself for not knowing the things you could not have known or predicted is priceless. Committing yourself to gaining knowledge so that you do not find yourself in a position of pain, fear, or sorrow again is priceless. These efforts are priceless because they help you escape the quicksand your body is submerged in.

But I cannot promise you that healing will fix everything, or that it will guarantee that nothing inconvenient, bad, or threatening happens to you ever again. **That is not how life works.** As much as you shoot for the stars, plan, and set systems, there will be curve balls. Remember that increasing flexibility in your line of thinking and recovery is essential because being adaptable prevents you from spiraling out of control.

Also, know that the challenges you face help you move the needle the most, but only when you *allow them* to do so. Only when you allow yourself to be vulnerable, transformed, and taught.

If you are going to do anything after reading this collection, I think it should be to heal your abrasions so that you can give yourself the life that you dream about. Without forgiving and letting go, you will constantly hunt for more, ruminate about the past, and stay stuck. HEAL.

BOUNDARIES

Caring for another person is selfless. It is bold, kind, and thoughtful. From your point of view, it may even feel necessary to take care of a struggling parent, a sibling who lost his or her way, or a close friend who is going through a tough divorce and needs a place to crash. I commend you for these things, but I also implore you to be mindful of your own needs. To be mindful of how the present moment is weighing on you.

Pay close attention to your feelings, emotions, thoughts, and energy. Ensure that your time, your absolute greatest asset, is not being compromised—and that you are not exchanging *your* goals completely in order to help someone else achieve *theirs*.

Know that as much as you want to be the peacemaker, or the saver, there is no such thing as saving someone who does not have an interest in being saved him or herself. This is a fact that you are going to have to accept. There is no such thing as changing someone for the better if that *"better"* does not align with his or her deepest values.

You cannot single-handedly do the inner work another person needs to do themselves—alone, on their own time—just because you care so much. And love so much.

I hope you continue to show love, always, and to be a support system to those you hold near and dear. However, I urge you to consider your boundaries and to stop crossing the line of turning selflessness into foolishness.

SELF-LOVE

Let yourself dance, especially in the rain. Stop letting the fear of a puddle splashing on your new dress and tarnishing it prevent you from going out into the elements. You may get dirty, and you may have to change afterwards, but what is worse—doing an extra load of laundry tomorrow, or completely missing a chance to live your life?

Your wings are not meant to stay stagnant. Nothing exciting, challenging, or rewarding comes from sitting still and avoiding growth. From creating excuse after excuse for why you cannot go to that concert, or wake up and hit the gym, or meal prep on Sunday afternoon so you can quit drowning your paycheck on lunch. The list of *"reasons"* is never-ending.

That is why, now more than ever before, I encourage you to set yourself free. Let yourself fly, even on the rainy days. Even on the days when the lightning and thunder pervade your conscious and dampen your mood.

No amount of darkness, pain, or fear can hold you in place unless you give it the power to do so.

ANOMALY

I know that there are days when you cannot stop interrogating yourself. When you struggle to find the courage to defy the rules, establish a new path, and stay consistent. There are days when it feels like nothing goes your way, too. When it feels like the universe is seriously conspiring against you. I know that there are days when you cannot find a way through, when there are more and more responsibilities piling up on your plate and less and less time to execute them. When you are losing a grip over your priorities and find yourself fading into toxic rituals.

It is on these very days that I hope you remember how miraculous you are.

It is on these days that I hope you remember how capable you are of controlling your emotions and responses, and of making smart decisions. *Choices that align with your vision and that make sense for your body, mind, and soul.*

Know that if something feels wrong, like it is tugging at your heart or causing an uneasiness within your stomach, you must trust your gut instinct. You must remember your power, too, because it is your response to these kinds of days that sets the tone for your assemblage.

It is all about the way you carry your anomalous self… it is all about self-control.

MOM

Thank you for holding me tight for all those long, painful years. For reminding me that I am worth it, even when I could not stop crying and had lost total faith in myself. Thank you for telling me that I deserve it all and that I can achieve whatever I set my mind to. Thank you for sharing your shortcomings, for teaching me about patterns you would never want me to repeat. Thank you for being vulnerable, truthful, and authentic with me. Thank you for pushing me towards what was best for me even if I did not see it as best suited in the moment.

Thank you for being such an undeniable source of inspiration, love, and motivation in my life.

Most of all, I cannot thank you enough for seeing my potential. And for identifying this potential, resting dormant beneath my delicate bones, before I could identify it within myself. Thank you for reminding me to stop forcing myself to fit in places where my energy was not welcomed. For constantly encouraging me and picking me back up after I fell, time and time again. For following me through the darkness until I woke up and the shadows ran away.

Rock bottom hits differently when there is someone like you to help me climb out of a dark hole. You have brought me here, to this remarkable, empowered, and enlightened place that I reside in today. Without your unconditional love, the long conversations, nighttime drives, and handholding, I know I would most definitely not be standing in this spot.

So thank you, Mom.

Thank you for being my guardian angel, my keeper, and my best friend.

PART 3

BUILDING

IN CONTROL

The day you become free is like the falling act of a movie after the drama has concluded. It is like the scene of your favorite show when the sun starts shining again.

I hope you know that you are more than capable of actualizing this day for yourself, too, because it is the day you stop placing your happiness in other people's control.

It is the day you take ownership over your life and get comfortable being your truest self. It is the day you cease caring so much about what other people think and go for it. It is the day you say no to plans you do not want to go through with. When you start loving every inch of your existence and genuinely enjoy taking yourself out on a dinner date, to the movies, and snuggling up in bed with a novel and a cup of peppermint tea. When you belt out the lyrics to your favorite song while cooking blueberry pancakes on Saturday morning.

Once you prioritize the relationship you have with yourself above all else, you can no longer be shaken.

Misaligned comments, roadblocks, and errant decisions cannot disrupt your mental peace and throw you off balance. In this state, your personal values—your personal worth—are rooted so deeply within you that they become inseparable components of your existence. In this state, you fully accept what makes you, YOU.

You are in control, and you are finally free.

TAKING CARE OF
YOURSELF

I hope you choose to take care of yourself *first* because you are enough just the way you are, and you deserve to feel loved, appreciated, and respected.

I hope you choose to hold your own hands in the face of adversity, live loudly, and always show love. To know that the only constant in life is change, and that if you do not learn to embrace it, you will flow in a constant state of fear, despair, dread, and anxiety. I hope you remind yourself that just because it works for your friends, or for your parents, or for your sister, does not mean it needs to work for you, too.

I hope you remember that confusion stems from a lack of awareness over your own inner narrative, and presents itself through dismay and irritability.

Know that building yourself up all over again will require an enormous amount of mental resilience. It will require a tenacious desire to bounce back from pain and honor yourself. It will demand an unwavering ability to see through hardships and it will test your foundation. So even when it is difficult, I hope you stay true to who you are and persistent in pursuit of your dreams.

We all fall, but when you believe in your unique purpose, you will have no problem picking yourself back up and remaining disciplined enough to *try, try, try* again.

RENTER

I hope you know that the longer you go without giving yourself an opportunity to embrace change, the harder it becomes to build a home within yourself.

The harder it becomes to get a hold of your thoughts and direct them in a more positive direction. The harder it becomes to change your trajectory, feel comfortable and at peace with who you are, and love yourself again.

The farther you move along without ever feeling at home within yourself.

The longer you let these dangerous behaviors last, the less and less of yourself you become. The longer you continue renting out space in a home that is not built *for* you, *by* you.

Know that the longer you rent, the longer your identity deteriorates, and that when you vibrate on this wavelength for enough time, **you forget who you are altogether**.

RECONCILE

This is a reminder that no one who is extremely successful, proud, satisfied, and pleased with him or herself got to that spot without hard work. And without a bunch of long nights, difficult conversations, and tough decisions.

The people who *"make it"* had the courage to put themselves out there and quelled their fear of failure.

Understand that the basis of all the *"hardness"* and *"difficulty"* you perceive in building your ideal self is not necessarily the actions or systems or doings themselves. The hardness and the difficulty are in defeating the voice in your head that instills so much apprehension within you. The very voice that causes you to miss your journey entirely because you are so scared of what failure feels like that you would rather not even try at all.

Giving in to this fear means your ego, your lowest self, your imposter, *wins*.

In doing so, you give up on the opportunity of a lifetime—one that requires sacrifice and discipline, of course, but one that totally transforms who you are. So please remind yourself that you are not the only person concerned about their aptitude. So many other people doubt themselves, too, but it is the ones who know how to reconcile their fears and move forward regardless of how loud the chaos is who see permanent results.

If you want to continue this self-assembly, you need to push yourself a little farther when the noise does everything in its power to keep you incapacitated.

SUCCUMB

If you are actively choosing to succumb to fear, I hope you evaluate the consequences first. And I hope you remember that running is simply a temporary fix to a larger issue.

I hope you also know that the moments of euphoria and numbness are ones that fuel your demons. Your monsters want you to stay down because that is where you do not have to be vulnerable or experience the pain of confession, evolution, and forgiveness.

In these periods of doubt, please remember your strengths. Realize just how powerful and capable you are of digging yourself out of whatever hole you think you are in right now.

NOT IMPOSSIBLE

T he only limit you have in life is the limit you place on your own thoughts.

If you believe it is impossible to face your fears, it will continue to be impossible until you break your mindset. It is not impossible unless you constantly tell yourself it is impossible. If you think you are destined for failure, you will be. Not because I said it, or because the world said it, or because your ex said it, but because you continue to shut light out and hibernate in the darkness. You continue to let what you *think* is real become your reality and disqualify yourself.

I hope that after reading this you bust open your shades, work through the aches, and prove to yourself that you are worth it.

TRANSITIONS

L et yourself be yourself.

Take responsibility for bringing your bravery, your smile, your brains, your athleticism, and your courage into this world. Also, know that you are better off doing so alone than conforming to a pack headed the opposite direction.

I truly want you to lead. I want you to take your future into your own hands. To stop following in the footsteps of those who have no business governing your path. Be wary of unsolicited advice that leaves you feeling more confused, unsure, and uncertain than you were beforehand. It is likely that the delegator of this guidance has lost him or herself as it is.

Please fall in love with the process of becoming more like yourself than you have ever been before. Fall in love with the early mornings, counseling sessions, and post-work walks, too.

Know that it is these incremental steps that come to define your assemblage—not the end of the journey, nor the feelings of relief or accomplishment that come along the way. It is the journey *itself* that forces you to get comfortable in the home you have constructed for yourself.

Embrace this transitory time and smile when you look back at how far you have come. Feel the weight being lifted off your shoulders as you let yourself fully be yourself and no longer fear stepping apart from the pack.

ABYSS

One day you will stop recognizing the woman staring back at you in the mirror because you know that she does not embody your principles. That woman is not reflective of your values or of your highest potential. At the same time, you have become so comfortable in your patterns that you struggle to adjust. There is so much fear and angst surrounding stepping outside of your comfort zone that you would rather live unhappily than do something about your situation.

Once you reach this point, you are faced with two options: resistance or transcendence.

Your livelihood weighs in the balance.

WITHIN YOU

I n case no one has told you this today: **you have what it takes.**

You are equipped to lift yourself from the ditch you are in right now and create a life you love waking up to every morning. It truly does not matter how many mistakes or wrong turns you have made so far. It does not matter if you did not graduate college, come from the brightest neighborhood, or have a staunch support system. These things will inevitably impact you, but they do not need to mandate your outcome. If you believe in yourself, and are willing to teach yourself what you need to know in order to elevate, know that you will make it.

Start believing that you have what it takes and coach, educate, and love yourself.

VALUE PROPOSITION

Maybe it is time for you to define your value proposition. Think of this as your WHY statement, as a representation for what you bring to the table for *yourself*. Not to attract others to you, satisfy the needs of your community members, or make your family proud.

Your value proposition is what makes you, **you**. It is why you are unique, why you have a purpose in this world, and what you offer to yourself.

As a byproduct, your value proposition may offer value to others, but in no way are your values defined by anything other than your own needs and desires. Start *intentionally* thinking about this concept:

- What makes you, you?

- What do you stand for?

- What do you enjoy doing?

- How do you need to be treated?

- What are your priorities?

Having these core tenets in mind will shape your actions, thought processes, and natural instincts. Above all, they will help you pinpoint your value—your **WHY**.

OVERCONFIDENCE

This is a reminder that arrogance and overconfidence kill your progress. In fact, these traits block you from making any real progress at all.

Instead of allowing yourself to acquire knowledge in a field you may not be that bright in, you will consistently convince yourself that what you do not know is not *important enough* for you to know.

This mindset, or rather, this lack of an optimistic, growth mindset, sets you so far back because you are not only preventing yourself from advancing, but you are also lying to yourself.

In a world full of liars, cheaters, and con artists, hear me when I say that the last thing you need to do is lie to yourself.

Please stop hiding your ignorance about a subject matter you really should know more about. Quit telling yourself that you know it all and that your learning is complete because knowledge is infinite.

If you are looking to learn something new every day, you will learn something new every day. On the contrary, if you are looking to stay the same, you will stay the same even as an abundance of information surrounds you. You will not ingest insights because your eyes are not open. This happens when you blind yourself to the sun's rays instead of absorbing light into your body.

When you catch yourself being arrogant and overconfident in your capabilities, I want you to read, have meaningful conversations, engage with your network, and listen to a podcast. Actions like these will lead you to a path of real progress.

VISUALIZATION

One of the simplest ways to become your highest self is to start visualizing her.

- What does she wear and what are her favorite foods, places, and books?

- How does she make an income—or better yet, how does she make multiple income streams?

- When does she feel most vulnerable, excited, and alive?

- Why does she treat others the way she does?

- Why does she feel inspired to rise from her bed every morning?

- Who is part of her inner circle?

Once you have these answers, you can sketch a map of the individual lying dormant within you. **By no means are you embodying someone who is not already alive within you, though.** You are simply pumping energy into digging her out from the fortress she is buried in. You are getting real on your values, priorities, and desires, and aligning them with your daily actions, thought patterns, and behaviors. You are accepting the fact that you have work to do to unearth the woman you have shut down for all these years.

Having this visualization in place also makes it much easier to ascertain your core principles, implement them into the *present*, and stop mulling them over without actually living them out.

EMPATHY

I hope you accept that no one will ever fully understand all the battles you have walked through. It does not matter how hard you beg them to show compassion for the turbulence you faced and hold you in a higher regard because of your story.

No one will ever be able to comprehend all that you lost, either. The sleepless nights, regret, pain, and anger. No one will ever be able to grasp what it was like to suffer for years. How tirelessly you fought to keep your head above water, help the ones you love most, and choreograph your life as it slowly slipped from your grip. They may show empathy, but they will never know how it feels to be you.

Because they are not you. *And that is okay.*

Just be proud of yourself for making it this far. For saving yourself and surviving all the bad days. You do not need anyone else's recognition, pity, or commendation to make it all worth it. You are worth it, and you matter, because you are you. You have transformed yourself so powerfully, become so much more yourself than ever before, and you are still here, wanting to improve and learn as much as humanly possible.

Please learn to be okay with the fact that no one will ever be able to appreciate the hardships you have endured as deeply as you can.

BEGGING YOU

I am begging you to *stop* begging people to stay in your life.

To stop asking them repeatedly to treat you the way you want to be treated. To stop giving chance after chance with little change in character. Stop making excuses for them and lying about their actions to your friends so that you do not have to hear their wrath. Do not convince yourself that it is all in your head and belittle yourself by thinking you are the problem when you are the farthest thing from it. Most of all, please stop begging people to live in accordance with your values and standards when clearly, their principles are not compatible with yours.

Be conscious of the tone in your voice, the beat in your chest, and the shaking in your hands as you hold on, tighter and tighter, to a person who is clearly not meant for you. See through the fog—the dense haze of love, lust, insecurity, and pleasure—that is clouding your judgment. This very fog is making it impossible for you to see the writing on the wall: **they are just not meant for you.**

Does that make them a bad person? Not necessarily.

But the more and more you beg for another person to stay, the less and less you honor yourself. You are so busy chasing someone who is not right for you that you are wasting all your energy (your greatest asset). This same energy could be placed into more profitable ventures like getting another degree, applying for an internship, working out, or spending time with loved ones who *actually care* about you.

Stop giving someone your all who has no intention of reciprocating the same energy.

I am begging you.

YOUR CIRCLE

I hope you choose to be very selective when it comes to your circle of friends, acquaintances, coworkers, and family members.

If your circle is not challenging, teaching, or inspiring you to become the highest version of yourself, I need you to stop thinking that you are the problem and to start considering who you are allowing access into your life. *Who are you letting suck up your time? Are they supportive of your growth plans?*

Evaluate your surroundings, specifically the lifestyles, values, and practices of your closest friends and family.

- Are these people on your wavelength?

- Do they bring out the best in you?

- Why do they treat you the way they do? Do they have corrupt intentions?

- Do they genuinely want what is best for you, or do they hold you back because they cannot stand to see you shine?

If you are realizing that your environment may not be benefiting you, have the courage to act. Position yourself for success by actively choosing to hang out with individuals who motivate you, accept you for who you are, and believe in your potential. There are so many bright, intelligent, caring, and kind individuals in the world, you just need to be willing to find them.

Be brave. Emerge from the fortress you are in today and develop an atmosphere that coincides with your most authentic self.

FAILURE

The only thing worse than failing is never trying at all. **You are better off putting yourself out there than you are holding yourself in the same comfortable enclave forever.** You are far better off testing your limits than you are accepting them as barriers that will perpetually inhibit you from growing beyond their existence.

Nothing exciting, new, or compelling happens when you stay in the same place. Absolutely nothing worth talking and jumping out of bed about in the morning happens when you keep yourself in gridlock. Holding yourself in the same routine that does not serve you for far too long is demoralizing.

But I do know that failure stinks. Not gaining acceptance to your dream school, getting cut from the team, and being declined a job opportunity are terrible feelings. They are embarrassing, make you feel worthless, and reinforce the concept you have put into your mind that you are not good enough. They validate that you will never achieve your intentions because you do not have what it takes.

In these moments, please examine the opportunities embedded *within* the failures instead of wallowing in defeat.

Maybe your failure presents you with a chance to modify and try again next time with a better mindset. Maybe the loss needed to happen. Without the slip-up, you would not know how to appreciate the wins. Maybe a no is not really a no, but a redirection that forces you to believe in yourself when no one else wants to believe in *you*.

Treat your failures as moments to rise because **failing is better than failing to try at all**.

ULTERIOR

Have you ever considered that maybe the people whose beliefs you value so strongly are insecure themselves?

- That they do not believe in themselves?

- That they struggle to look at the reflection staring back at them in the mirror?

- That they question their motives, passions, and dreams?

- That they never felt loved or appreciated in childhood, and that their scars have stuck with them?

- That maybe, just maybe, they are taking their frustration and lack of self-confidence out on you by bringing you down with them?

- That they purposefully make subtle gestures, statements, and poorly timed comments so that you doubt yourself?

- That they want you to feel insecure, unworthy, and unable to achieve your dreams because that is exactly how they feel?

- That sabotaging any effort you take to enhance your reality is their sole prerogative?

Realize that you are allowing people who are dissatisfied with themselves to shake you. That not everyone has it all figured out, and that the picture-perfect profiles you see on your screen do not accurately represent the people smiling back at you.

Please stop basing your life decisions on the lectures and advice of others. Stop asking for opinions from people who are not educated enough to guide you in the direction that is right for *you*. Not one that is right for them, or for society, or for their child, or for their younger self.

The further you migrate from this flawed mindset, the more often you will shake your head and cringe at the fact that you ever valued another being's perspective over your own.

OBSERVATION

Remember that one of the most powerful tools at your disposal does not cost any money. And it is something we are all born with, but do not use enough. **It is observation.**

The closer you review and analyze meaningful situations, mistakes, and lessons, the more you can learn, adjust your path, and move on with a refined outlook. I want you to focus on building your observation muscle because the more you practice, the stronger your instincts get.

I hope you take the time to understand *why* you may have slipped up at your last job instead of convincing yourself that all your shortcomings are due to external factors since you are perfect exactly as you are. None of us are perfect, and part of enabling growth is observing. These two practices go hand in hand: through observation, you birth your own core pillars and values. The knowledge you obtain teaches you just as much about what you *do* want as it does about what you do *not* want.

With these takeaways in hand, you can set a strategy for implementing behaviors, customs, and routines that closely align with your principles. **This is where the magic starts.** This is where the growth starts, where you gain the ability to reset your system and build back better than ever. This is the moment that you catapult farther than ever before.

Using observation as a tool to unlock your success helps you see the world from a much more open-minded and educated stance. It helps you assemble.

DISLIKES

As you take a deep breath in, remain mindful of the air wafting its way through your nostrils. *Refreshing. Replenishing.*

Remain mindful of the oxygen it supplies your blood with so that you can execute your day. Of how it supports, sustains, and supplies you with the necessary elements of life.

Now, exhale and release all the toxicity, sadness, pain, danger, lost love, negativity, and hate.

You will find that these things expend themselves at lightning speed because they are eager to escape a body they are not meant to live in.

Understand that maybe the things you hate most about yourself will find a loving home in someone else's body. Maybe someone else enjoys the things you dislike. Know that this is proof enough that realizing what you do not want does not make you bad or unlikable—it just shows that these opinions make you, you.

Maybe getting rid of things that are not meant for you opens space for what *is*. This act replaces the emptiness you feel inside your soul... a soul full of the wrong content.

LOST

An unpopular opinion: **it is okay to feel lost.**

Learn to accept uncertainty as an opportunity for evolution instead of breaking down. Panicking, projecting your thoughts into the past and future, telling yourself that you are always one step behind, and believing that your confusion invalidates you really jeopardizes you.

Know that it is only in the moment when you do not know where to turn next that you are given an endless stream of possibilities. You expose yourself to the unknown: you could go anywhere, start any project, join any organization, and make any decision. This leads you to another string of decisions, and then to another, and then another.

There is no wrong path, either; there is just the path you are on and how you choose to adapt when you find out that path is no longer serving your best interests.

Lostness is just finding your way back home. It is discovering what defines you and reinventing. It is all these things and more, even though the original feeling of being lost is disguised as alarming, endangering, and hazardous.

SELF-ACCEPTANCE

One of the greatest pleasures you can award yourself in life is the pleasure of feeling comfortable in your own skin. Of dedicating yourself *to* yourself.

It is only when you make the decision to pay attention to yourself, partake in me-time, and be at peace alone that you demonstrate real progress. When you do not mind going shopping as a party of one, sitting in the library by yourself, and posting pictures that genuinely bring you joy, you feel empowered in your own skin. When you stop obsessing over a digital world that is in no way reflective of what you have in the present moment, you feel rejuvenated. Once you reach this level, you can motivate others to love themselves, too, and that is the real prize.

I hope you learn to love who you are by toning out the critics, bullies, and noise. I hope you also forgive yourself and assemble your inner narrative because if you cannot do that today, no one else will do it for you. **You will continuously struggle to make any real advancement in life.**

DEADLINES

You are not on a hard deadline.

There may be deadlines at your job, or in your degree program, but in life, there are no deadlines unless you enforce them upon yourself. So go easy on yourself when you need a little extra love and remember that your pace is just that: YOURS.

GROW THROUGH IT

G row through what you go through.

Grow through heartbreaks, letdowns, and terrible experiences. Use the frustration, disappointment, and fear as educational moments. Please do not treat them as dead ends. Do not allow your shortcomings to define you, either, because they are not capable of doing such a thing. The only way these components restrict you is if you let them. *It is all in your mindset.*

Know that growth is not always fun, convenient, or easy, but in the process, you uncover the potential buried deep inside of you. You see just how much creative genius rests dormant within you.

Remember that it takes a lot of bravery, strength, and emotional resiliency to choose yourself. To build yourself up and evolve in a world that makes you feel like progress is so far out of reach and falsely labels you as selfish for doing so. Taking these growth strides is worth it because you become much more like yourself than you have ever been before, and that is all that truly matters.

AUTHENTICITY

A uthentic... being who you are, unapologetically. Real. Genuine. Honest. True. *"Of undisputed origin"* (Oxford Languages).

In a world where authenticity is rare, I hope you choose yourself. I hope you choose to honor yourself and to live out your truth no matter the support you receive, or whether it is a popular decision, or whether it ignites a terror within you like no other.

Stop placing so much emphasis on what others think of you, especially those who have never met the real you. Cease placing so much importance on conforming to the norms, meeting expectations, accepting circumstances as unchangeable, and keeping your voice low. None of these acts relieve your stress, bring you joy, or help you develop. They simply crush your spirits, dull your self-esteem, and give others the opportunity to walk all over you like a front doormat.

Remember that the only view that matters in this life is the view you have of yourself.

That this approval, confidence, and perspective sets the tone for your behavioral patterns. That it sets the tone for how you present yourself in this world and whether you see yourself in a positive light. It sets the tone for the way you carry and treat yourself, too.

In a world where authenticity is rare, please let your truest yourself run wild.

TREASURE

reasure the little moments in life.

Treasure the early mornings when the world is still silent, and you can actually hear yourself think. When you find a parking spot in a crowded lot. When you crawl into bed with freshly made sheets after a long day, and when a stranger gives you a soft smile. When the sun sets and the sky morphs into a purple, pink, and orange glow.

I want you to treasure the little moments in life because one day you are going to look back and realize that they had a profound impact on your direction.

I truly hope you make the shift from living in the past, or in the future, to living fully in the present. I hope you take note of your thoughts, too. Describe what catches your eye as you walk down the street. Notice how you react to new environments—whether they excite you or bring you anguish. Know that these indicators teach you how much you are valuing the present moment.

It is the little things—the moments you too often discount—that matter the most. They may not present themselves as unique or showstopping, but that is ultimately what makes them so significant. They embody you by exemplifying the day-to-day occurrences of your life.

PATIENCE IS A VIRTUE

If you struggle with being patient, I hope you remind yourself that nothing worth having comes quickly or easily. That rushing a natural process only postpones your results, making it less likely that you will achieve all your objectives.

It is solely when you walk with patience and do not yearn for immediate results that you feel proud walking across the finish line. You put in the work. You waited your turn, had faith in yourself, your purpose, and your journey. You worked tirelessly and pushed onwards. You coached yourself through the bumps and talked yourself out of poor decisions.

When the frustration mounts, because it inevitably will, I want you to keep telling yourself that patience is a virtue. That having patience allows you to glorify your journey. **That all good things worth possessing come in time.**

DETOURS

uilding a home within yourself does not mean that you need to have it all figured out. That you need to know exactly how your life is going to play out over the next two to five years. It does not mean that you need a specific roadmap in place, and it most certainly does not mean that you are a failure if you do not meet your own lofty expectations.

Understand that getting started *is* enough. Promising yourself that you will put yourself first no matter what *is* enough. It is enough for me, and it should be enough for you, too.

In this ever-changing world, know that there is no way you could possibly have every detail of your life planned out. Despite your best intentions and vivid fantasies, it is not realistic. Hurdles will arise, resources will deplete, and your goals may very well change, too.

Please be okay with the fact that you are never going to have all the answers—this is part of the beauty in taking the leap. You are giving yourself the power to adapt, to become whoever it is you need to become in order to fit your circumstances and respond to your highest calling. You are trusting that, although you have a framework and guideposts in place to mark your course, some days you will color outside the lines. It is on these very days, however, when you recognize the power in venturing a little farther off path than originally planned.

Detours only motivate you to find your way back home again. **Back to your truest self.**

SOCIAL MEDIA IS NOT ALWAYS REAL

What if listening to all your favorite influencers on social media harms your mental health? What if emulating vloggers whose lives are polished and highly edited makes you hate your own life even more than you would have if you never consumed their content in the first place? What if you are discouraged by the fact that you can never look like or act like the models on your feed? What if subscribing to a bunch of podcasts or accounts that promote unrealistic expectations makes you question everything about yourself?

Have you ever asked yourself what would happen if you stopped?

1. What would happen if you turned your phone off, shut out the noise, and lived FOR you?

2. What would happen if you recognized that your social media screen time may very well endanger your health?

3. What would happen if you took ownership over ending the cycle of comparison and anguish you subject yourself to?

4. What would happen if you stopped listening to and reading about how to change your life, start your business, or launch your product, and *actually did it?*

This is just a reminder that the only life that matters is the one you wake up to every morning—not the ones your favorite content creators select to share with you on their stories, reels, or live streams.

Until you differentiate between these digital displays of a curated reality and the reality you are facing, you will continue to hurt. You will continue to degrade your emotional, intellectual, and physical health.

HOLD THEM

I f you truly care for someone and want to make them a part of your life, you owe it to yourself to do so.

I think that you should make the sacrifices necessary to keep the people who make you feel alive and whole—the ones who provoke your soul—close to home.

I think if life has shown us anything in the past few years, it is that isolation is *real*. Separation is damaging, and being apart from the ones who mean the most to you by sheltering yourself out of civilization does not make things any easier. It does not defend you from sadness, grief, or disappointment. Forcing yourself into your own box only worsens your health, morale, and confidence.

Know that the world needs people to lean on, and the world most definitely needs more people like *you* in it.

As you move your way through whatever transformation you are going through, I truly hope you remember to make space, time, and energy for the ones who support you. A little guidance, and a lot of love, is what makes the hard times a little less challenging. Loyal people are the ones who share in your happiness, success, and short-comings. Please remember to hold onto them and to treat them with the same kindness and respect you show yourself.

I AM SORRY

I am sorry that the world made you feel so cold.

I am sorry the world showed you its darkest sides and made you doubt yourself far too often.

I am sorry that the world destroyed your resolve and broke your heart.

I am sorry that the world made you feel like you were incapable of being loved. Like you were never a good enough friend and like you never had a safe space to call your own.

I am sorry this world caused you immense harm by placing you in compromising positions—especially the harmful childhood events that destroyed your confidence and left you with lingering traumas.

I am sorry the world did not give you whatever you were looking for all those years.

I am sorry for the lost loves, deaths, untimely sicknesses, and challenges that slowly chipped away at you.

I am sorry that you had to go through all of this alone.

I hope you can celebrate the wins and the good times you have had, though. I hope you can recognize just how courageous you are, and I hope you are proud of yourself for surviving. For giving it your all and not letting the weak moments and invisible scars characterize you. I hope you choose to forgive yourself for not knowing any better and for electing to move forward.

THE CRASH

One day, the people, situations, occupations, and connections that are not meant for you are going to come crashing down. I hate to be the first one to break it to you, but the crash itself is going to burn a hole inside of you like no other. It will do so because you hold on so rigidly to things that are not in harmony with the direction you are *headed*. They seem so fun, perfect, fitting, and exciting right now, but as you grow, you surpass things that are not meant for you.

It is only human.

Understand that while these things may morph themselves into components that can fit your altered composition, they will not last long because they will bring about reminders of a life you used to live. Of a past you have already moved on from. Of a lifestyle you now despise and of a woman you no longer resemble.

As much as parting ways with these things burns, it opens space for you to adopt new people, skill sets, and hobbies into your world.

Think of it as a burning event that doubles as a clearing act.

Trust that the universe has your back, and that everything happens *for* you *for* a reason. Even if it is impossible to see in the moment, it will all work itself out because it is all happening to bring you closer to where you truly need to be.

BET ON YOU

Maybe life is less about existing in accordance with the template society creates for you, and more about being brave enough to define your own terms and **bet on yourself.**

Your life is not about continuous conformity. It is about having the courage to venture down the road less traveled, trust your instincts, and abnegate hesitation.

Maybe life is meant to be led, not followed—bet upon, not shied away from.

Shoved

People are going to shove you in the direction that makes sense for *them*.

The world is full of people who thrive on giving their two cents about everyone else's lives. They relish the chance to incorrectly judge other people's progress without even knowing enough about them to accurately do so.

This makes it even more important to know yourself and dream. To have values in place that anchor you to the right feelings, mindsets, and people. It makes it more important to know who you are and what you stand for, and to uphold your ideals regardless of your mood.

When you are firm in your existence, you are less susceptible to being sculpted by the crowd. You are less prone to flip-flopping, or trying out a job just because your friend said so, or changing your major because your mom thought it would be a good idea. **When you know you, you know what will work for you.**

When you do not know you, however, you continue allowing the opinions of others to shove you down paths that lead you to places you have no interest in traversing.

DEPTH

Prioritize connections, conversations, and individuals who provide depth and not fluff. As you build your home, commit to only letting your body absorb what makes you feel whole. What brings new perspectives, eye-opening experiences, and concepts into your world, and what changes you for the better.

Please stop feasting on the words, promises, and wishes of those who have no intention of fulfilling the stories spewing from their mouths. Learn from the negativity that consumed your body in the past. Most of all, remember that complexity brings an enriching factor into your life by emboldening your world with knowledge and insights. Depth and substance fill you up; on the other hand, fluff is deceiving and useless. It is inherently false, and it is not worth your energy.

LEARNED THIS WAY

P lease know that the most resilient human beings were not born with a rare, genetic capability to conquer hardships. They did not come straight out of the womb on a mission to save themselves, time and time again.

The most resilient human beings *became* that way because they know exactly what it feels like to suffer.

They know exactly what it is like to feel worthless, lost, confused, and anxious.

They know exactly what it feels like to lose their friend group, have their heart broken, and walk alone.

They know exactly what it is like to always be the one left behind, to feel out of place, be made fun of, and excluded from plans.

They know exactly what it feels like to wander down the harder path—the one filled with hurdles and jumps that none of their peers had to take.

They know exactly what it feels like to have the world ripped right out from underneath them and to feel uncomfortable in their own home.

They know exactly what it is like to plead for someone else's approval and time.

They know exactly what it feels like to lose themselves to the chaos.

They also know exactly what it feels like to redeem themselves.

They know what the power of healing feels like. They know what the power of reclaiming their inner voice feels like, too.

Please understand that the most resilient souls became that way—*they were not born with it*. Because of this fact, you have the potential to become one of them.

THE REASON WHY

When you find yourself feeling discouraged, remind yourself that everyone comes into and out of your life for a reason. That there is a larger purpose behind your struggles, heartaches, letdowns, and lost loves.

Every single random occurrence, and every single human being that has been a part of your world, played a role in creating the individual you are today.

- Where would you be if you stayed home that night instead of attending your friend's birthday party... you would have never met *him*.

- Where would you be if you went to a different college, if you missed that flight to Chicago, or if you did not take the leap and make it happen for yourself?

Know that your life is defined by the small movements that end up compromising the bulk of your existence and molding your perspectives. As such, I hope you know that when you question what is going on in your life, and curse the world for putting you through another obstacle course, you are really inching closer and closer to finding out who you are.

It is only by keeping your eyes wide open, and soaking up lessons like a sponge, that you experience growth. **It is only when you allow knowledge, emotion, and experience to seep into your soul that you can awaken your highest self.**

I SEE YOU

I see you. *I can see all of you.*

I see the way you avoid rush hour trains in fear of bumping into him.

I see the way you carry yourself.

I see the pain you have been grappling with.

I see the exhaustion written right across your face.

I see the regret you possess for not making smarter choices when you were younger.

I see how hard you fought to pull yourself out of whatever ditch you found yourself in, although you did not make as much progress as you would have liked.

I see the sleepless nights and remorse.

I can see all of you because I relate to you.

I know what it feels like to have nowhere else to turn. I know what it feels like to want to give up, to feel ashamed, embarrassed, and devoid of hope. I know what it feels like to be ignored, constantly rejected, and put in situations you were far too young to experience.

I also know that until you stop believing that you are the only one who went through challenging times, you will never be able to unclog your brain. You will never be able to save yourself because you are so busy tossing and turning over erasing an *inerasable* past.

Please let people in. Give yourself the chance to grow. Know that your past does not need to define you, and that realizing you are unhappy is simply an occasion for renovation.

Know that having no other direction to turn means you must turn within first.

DESPERATION

Desperation. *"A state of despair, typically one which results in rash or extreme behavior"* (Oxford Languages).

Have you ever wondered why human beings wait until they are absolutely desperate and have no other option before they do something about their situation? Why they need impending doom to threaten them before they make the changes they should have made six months ago?

Maybe it is that they do not feel motivated enough until there is nowhere else to turn. Or maybe it is that they do not feel pressured enough until their current state of despair is blatantly unsustainable.

Remember that human beings are inherently anti-change. They are not inclined to uproot their lives and start over because that is perceived as being too hard, difficult, and time-consuming. Even when things are not going their way, and they feel overwhelmed, unsafe, and unhappy, they rarely choose to do anything about it.

But not you.

You will not let desperation dictate your life. You are smarter than that and you are not like the rest—you are ready to own your future. You are ready to give yourself an improved, value-driven life, and you will not quit until you achieve your intentions.

Above all, you are not willing to flirt with the chance of hitting rock bottom again. You know better and you will act wiser because of this.

PROTECT YOURSELF

Please take it upon yourself to protect your energy because your energy is your everything.

It is what motivates you to complete your to-do list. It is what recharges you after a long day of work or a night out with your closest friends. It carries you throughout your workouts and keeps you company when you feel like crying, too.

Know that your energy is sacred, and that you are entirely in control of what you expend it on. Because of this fact, I hope you choose to keep enough for yourself. To set boundaries, say no, and remind your co-workers and family members of your obligations.

Remember that people who genuinely care for you want to be a part of your life. They will respect you for who you are and will not care if you tell them that you need a break. Or that you have had a long week and just need time alone. **Those who matter will not mind, and those who mind *do not matter.***

Please elect to give yourself all the attention, love, and kindness you constantly dole out to everyone else. Your body needs energy pumped back into it so it can operate at its optimum level.

PEAK PERFORMANCE

O f all the things you should already know about yourself, one of the most significant ones is that when you are at your peak, you can help others reach their peaks, too. When you feel content with who you are, confident in your own skin, and eager to live to the fullest extent, that aura radiates off you. It enables you to give, teach, and empower.

Reaching a place of happiness and strength within yourself is significant not only because it is a personal win, but because it is a win for society. Once you perform at your highest potential, you can guide your family and peers to success, transformation, and growth as well. You become a microcosm for all that is right in this world. You are given the power to modify the rulebook, bring your loved ones out of the shadows, and preach your message. On top of all that, when you are at your peak, you can consistently take care of yourself.

So if nothing more, know that your journey will give itself back to you.

It will give itself back to the day one supporters and to those captivated by your bravery, too. It will provide an example for others to observe and mimic. It will elicit hope for those certain they are destined for the dumps. It will offer inspiration for your acquaintances, and it will also create a platform from which you can share, collaborate, and spread your gifts.

OFF PLAN

Sometimes your plans are not going to go according to plan. Sometimes, they are going to take you in a million different directions, throw you off balance, and make you frustrated. They are going to push your patience, stress you out, and cause you to wonder why you got started in the first place.

This is because a plan is simply that: *a plan*.

Know that there is no reality to a plan. There is no guarantee to a plan, either, because you are dealing with life, and life is unpredictable. There is no way to know what will happen, who will come in and out, and what unforeseen circumstance will throw a wrench in your ideas. This is the beauty of being human, of being adaptable, and of giving yourself the chance to evolve.

Know that even if your plans erupt like a boiling volcano, there is no shame in following your dreams. Pursuing your calling and taking a shot at whatever keeps nagging at you is *always* worth it because even if you fail, you will have honored your truth in the process.

Please have the courage and determination to keep going. Grind even when your plans are no longer useful or attainable because it is in the tough times that you learn to rise. **That you become the highest version of yourself.**

EVOLUTION

E volving is not the equivalent of failure. **I need you to drill this into your mind.**

Deciding to architect a life you can be proud of does not mean that the way you are living right now is a failure. That you are a waste, a directionless, meaningless, hopeless being. Making the decision to transform yourself does not mean that you need to morph into a brand-new person who is completely unrecognizable from the old you, either. And it definitely does not mean that you need to become more like your favorite celebrity, roommate, or best friend.

Evolving is simply *eliminating* the disturbances that keep you up at night. It is *elevating* your world while incorporating practices, routines, individuals, partnerships, and hobbies that bring you happiness, love, and joy. It is *changing* the pieces of you that are no longer harmonious with your values. It is *constructing* a home that reflects the components of yourself you love the most. It is *giving* yourself the opportunity to act on your potential and become the person you know you were always meant to be.

So no, embarking on this self-development journey does not mean that you are terrible the way you are right now. It means that you know that concentrated efforts will only help you become more of yourself than you have ever been before. It means you know that you can reverse course and start fresh.

TIME ASSESSMENT

K now that there is no such thing as something taking up too much time that you genuinely care about making time for. There is also no such thing as struggling to find time or pencil time into your schedule. There is no such thing as not having enough time in the day, either, because when you truly value something, **you make the time for it.**

When you really care about making something work, you will make the sacrifices necessary to actualize it. If you want to write a book, you will block out a few hours each week to dedicate towards pounding out the pages. If you want to go to fitness classes three times a week and get in shape, you will find time to attend your one-hour sessions. If you want to read twenty pages a day, you will find crevices of time to read twenty pages a day—if, and only if, it really matters to you.

Understand that it is not about being too busy, overbooked, or strapped for time. **It is about filling your calendar with things that incite a fire within your soul.** It is about making the time and the sacrifices for the necessary components of your world.

This is the only solution to your perceived lack of ability to *"fit it all in."* Know that you are in control, and that you will find the time. You will reorient to work smarter and move wiser.

FORGIVENESS

S ometimes, the hardest person to forgive in life is yourself.

It is seemingly impossible to get over your mistakes.

It feels like your failures pile up so quickly that there is no way out of the grief.

You are so ashamed and embarrassed of yourself for not knowing any better. You hold yourself to such high standards that it becomes virtually impossible to reconcile errors.

You were raised better than that. You should know better than that, yet you do not know better than that. You continue to slip up. You take a wrong turn, let down a friend, offend a stranger, and hurt a loved one's feelings.

You already know that you are wrong, though. You are just holding such a thick grudge that it is not only stagnating your growth, but also holding you in a state of despair. It is destroying your self-esteem and preventing you from loving yourself for who you are.

Please forgive yourself and move forward. Learn, change, and apologize when needed because exonerating yourself is the only way to suppress the commotion.

IT WILL PASS

I can promise you that whatever is invading your conscious right now will pass. You will overcome the heartbreak and the loss because nothing is permanent. *Nothing.*

I know that it does not feel that great right now, though. I see the pain that you are carrying in your heart. I know how much you wish for a better life and how hard you work to overcome your limitations. I see the worry that is written across your face. I see how damaging this experience has been on your confidence as well. I know that you are feeling dizzy at the thought of all the fights, betrayals, loneliness, and fatigue.

You can move past this all, though, because you are in charge.

You are in charge, and when your tears evaporate, know that their purpose will have been to rid your body of all the negativity—of all the things that were not meant for you in the first place. The pain, fear, and mistakes.

As such, I hope you choose to remind yourself, over and over and over again, that you will be okay. That this will pass because your life is defined by forward movement. You are meant to evolve, and the only way to successfully transform is to move beyond the situations you have already outdone. Let yourself feel and then *let go.*

PROCRASTINATION

"*The action of delaying or postponing something*" (Oxford Languages).

One of the smartest ways to outsmart procrastination is by telling yourself that the sooner you start doing something, the sooner it will be over.

The sooner you start your homework, the sooner you will not have any homework to do. The sooner you start taking classes towards your major, the sooner you can graduate, work, and get paid. The sooner you eat your greens, the sooner you can eat your potatoes. The sooner you start taking driver's education courses, the sooner you can have your license, drive to the beach, and grab your favorite sandwich all summer long.

If you are the type of person who constantly holds off on doing burdensome chores, please incorporate this approach. Ask yourself what it would feel like if that test, discussion board post, essay, or five-mile run was done. *Invigorating? Liberating? Thrilling?*

Now ask yourself why you are delaying that emotion you just came up with.

I hope you remember that inaction leads nowhere, and that holding off on living decelerates growth. That overcoming procrastination is less about being overly productive, and more about making short-term sacrifices in the *now* so that you can soak in the feeling of being done in the *future*.

TWENTYSOMETHINGS

Your early twenties are an era of massive change. Think about the:

- Friendships

- Life changes

- Graduation

- Bills

- Professors

- Lost loves

- First move out

- Post-graduation adjustment

- Full-time job

- Mistakes

- Last night of college

There are so many switches, yet so much falls into place as these switches occur; therefore, maybe it is time to be okay with the irregularities—with the situations you will be thrown into. Maybe it is time to be okay with not being okay.

It is time to be okay with feeling unprepared in your twenties, too. It is time to be okay with feeling like you are losing yourself or like your world is shifting so quickly, you can hardly keep up. You probably *are* losing yourself, and your world *is* most certainly evolving.

You are becoming.

You are gaining new responsibilities, tasks, and relationships. You are moving across the country, interviewing for your first full-time position, and going back to school for another degree. Your peers are also moving in their own special ways at the exact same time, so please make light of these natural changes. Give yourself the chance to appreciate your twenties while you are still living in them.

VULNERABLE

In case no one has told you this before, **vulnerability reflects your deepest self.**

Vulnerability is defined as *"the quality or state of being exposed to the possibility of being attacked or harmed, either physically or emotionally"* (Oxford Languages).

In a vulnerable state, you can metamorphose into a person who loves herself fully. You can gain the wisdom and clarity to do better in the future. You can overcome whatever leaves you feeling sorry for yourself and finally transform.

You can do all these things and more because vulnerability is a chasm of the things that scare you and make you feel most alive.

YOUR FUNDAMENTALS

Define your fundamentals. See them as the structures that prevent you from generating a sinking, unsupported foundation. See them as integral in fostering long-term growth—the kind of growth that remains with you throughout the highs and lows. **The kind of growth that awakens your most authentic self.**

Know that once you gain precision surrounding your fundamentals, you can venture beyond the norms, too. You can adopt new rituals, enhanced routines, and grander targets.

PAYING ATTENTION

I hope that you strive to pay attention in life. That you soak it all in, and that you put an end to aimlessly and carelessly drifting throughout your days.

I hope that you notice buildings being constructed in your neighborhood. That you check out that deal going on at the supermarket next week, or that kind gentleman who waved to you in the coffee shop, or the summer sun beating across your face. That you try to be polite, spread positivity, and show people that you care, because human beings come together when they feel accepted, appreciated, and respected for who they are.

I also hope that you choose to be the bigger person, because treating others the way you would like to be treated is far more important than anything else. Giving off the same energy and emotion you wish to have bestowed upon you is, too, so go a few minutes out of your way to drop an iced coffee off at your friend's house when you know she is having a rough day. Remember to text them happy birthday. Shovel your grandparents' driveway after a big snowstorm. Send postcards to the ones you love most while you are backpacking across Europe.

Showing people that you care does not need to be that difficult, but it *is* something you need to actively do. Not only will it make you feel better about yourself, but it will open your eyes to new ways of showing affection in this naturally selfish world.

It will prove that you are paying attention.

THE GIRL I USED TO BE

Maybe it is time to handle yourself with grace. To keep your head up high instead of resenting yourself for falling behind.

It is time to delve into your dreams, too. It is time to stop cursing your past for setting you back because if anything, your story has given you the tools and the motivation to disrupt the world. To unsettle whatever industry you work in and to uproot the cycle your family members consistently fall into. It has lit a ravenous fire inside of you that compels you to conquer any object or situation in your way. **It has given you your power because you did not go through all of your pain for nothing.**

Understand that there is a much larger meaning behind your struggles, behind the moments when you considered leaving yourself to rot. Behind the times you did not think you would make it through.

Know that you went through hell so that you could teach others how to avoid making similar mistakes. You went through misery so that you could become a better version of yourself. You went through it so that you could make more intelligent decisions in the future and so that you could inspire others to do the same.

You need to stop letting your past interfere with your present, and you need to stop feeling sorry for yourself. You are absolutely brilliant (and better off) because of the sadness you endured growing up. Until you assure yourself of this fact, you will always feel resentment towards the girl you used to be.

PART 4
INSTALLING

THIS IS WHERE YOU INSTALL

You have altered your surroundings to reflect your values and mesh with your intentions.

You have taken the time to cultivate your seeds.

You have set a strong, well-educated foundation, upon which you have assembled a framework for delineating who you are.

You are nearing the final stages of this transformative chapter in your life.

Please be proud of yourself for all that you have done to get to this point. Know that evolution is not a straightforward task, but that you are a fighter. That you have proven to yourself that you have what it takes to stay committed to your goals. **That you are ready to move into installation.**

Installation is the part where you put on the roofing, siding, front door, and other essential components that turn your structure into a livable space. This is where you demarcate what it means to feel content with this period of your life. You decide exactly how you want to spend your time, where you want to live, who you want to include in your plans, and what objectives, demeanors, and patterns best support your lifestyle. This is where you must remain persistent and finish out the journey that you have been working on for a long, long time. This is where you must become more compassionate and establish empowering feedback loops.

This is where the exciting part begins.

TWO FEET

As you install healthy coping skills and mindset habits into your world, I hope you remember that the moment you identify one as being unhealthy or toxic, **you need to act**. You need to call yourself out, get a grip, and reinvent your ways so that your hard work is not abandoned.

Do not get complacent and allow the act to fester and boil over into a much larger issue. Do not turn a blind eye and tell yourself that it will get easier with time, or that your dangerous coping mechanism is better than whatever you were doing to yourself beforehand.

Permitting yourself to believe these things is the opposite of progress. It is the furthest thing from what you strove to achieve when you put all this effort into transforming.

If you are going to step into your truth, please step into it with **two feet**. Not with your baby toe touching the outer edge of the pond. Go all in. Be brave.

POSITIVE FEEDBACK

G ive yourself positive feedback.

Frame your comments in ways that energize and teach you, as opposed to in ways that cripple your self-esteem. Even if you are disappointed with the way you acted, treat the experience as a lesson that can reform future behavior as opposed to believing that it is the end of the world. Learn to be okay with the fact that you will mess up and need to adjust.

This is all part of your installation.

FIRMNESS

B e firm in your decision to transform because transformation changes your life. Do not turn back when you hit a thorny bump, as these bumps will always be there and there is no changing that fact. No matter what you think you will accomplish, you will never put the bumps in their place because they cannot be redirected or eradicated. They are natural and they need to be tackled instead of fought against.

Remember that the only person you have complete control over is yourself. With this in mind, you must cease flip-flopping back and forth at the first sign of trouble. You must also let your plans run their course and give in to the unknown.

You must live a little looser, a little lighter, and a little freer.

You will find that once you give yourself firm consent to stray beyond the black and white, uncharted waters appear. They exceed expectations and they are the very waters that make the tough choices worth every second of debate.

Please do not fall back into patterns that did not serve you *then*, and will never serve you *now*.

NIGHT VERSUS DAY

N ight will always be followed by day. The two are undeniably linked: one cannot exist without the other. *Exact opposites.*

As such, you cannot experience calm without chaos. You cannot know joy and excitement without knowing pain and suffering. Appreciating light is impossible without knowing what it feels like to sit alone in darkness.

Remember that whatever end of the spectrum you are on right now is inevitably teaching you to *understand* the exact opposite emotion, too.

Once you become conscious of these poles, you will also gain a deeper awareness of your emotions. You will become much more thankful for the opportunities life awards you to reset and experience inverses.

Finally, know that there are two sides to every coin. And that being stuck in night for a while does not rule out the possibility of daylight pouring into your soul. With lots of inner work and a willingness to change, you can rouse the potential hiding within you.

FLEXIBILITY

In case you need to hear this today: being flexible is essential to making any real progress.

A lack of flexibility will leave you feeling so regimented and frustrated that you can hardly move forward without distractions. Your mind will constantly revert to how things *"should have"* been going. You will regularly compare yourself to where you told yourself you *"would be"* at this point, and since you are not there yet, you will initiate a pity cycle.

You will make yourself feel terrible for missing the mark, skipping a workout because you needed the sleep, and canceling your appointments because you were sick. You will blame others for your misfortunes and humiliate yourself for failing to achieve perfection.

Remember that you can never be perfect, though. Perfection is a myth, and it locks you into a scary pattern of setting your expectations far too high. You need to be okay with the fact that a perfect world only exists in your head. And that a little bit extra of this or that will not have a major impact on your overall direction.

Be realistic and flexible with yourself. Honor your desires and serve your needs. Have fun as you grow, even if that means sometimes your days will not be as productive as you may have wished, because guess what? *You get to try all over again tomorrow.*

MESSAGE TO MY YOUNGER SELF

The things I would have told my younger self if I had the chance:

1. Your circumstances are temporary, and because of this fact, they will not last forever. Learn to let them be and love yourself *despite* them.

2. Life is going to change a whole lot in your twenties, so if you try to remain stuck, life will uproot you and force you to change anyway.

3. **It is much more calming to initiate change yourself than to feel like the universe is tugging you to do so.**

4. Your GPA, outfit, hair, social media presence, job, relationship, makeup, friends, major, male attention, and past do not define you, **and they never will**.

5. The feelings, opinions, and ultimatums of other people simply **do not matter** unless they serve a purpose in your life.

6. Time flies. If you never slow down to acknowledge it, it will be gone before you know it.

7. You need to make the scariest decisions because you *earn* the most from them.

8. Stop caring so much about what other people think—and depending on what they think to make you feel a certain way about yourself.

9. **Release the heaviness.**

10. You are never going to change someone who does not want to change themselves.

11. Fear, doubt, and a lack of self-confidence are the same exact emotion expressed in different forms.

12. If you want to fly, you are going to have to discard the people, connections, and situations holding down your wings. This process is scary, and unlike anything you have done before, but you will be okay.

13. You are capable.

14. If you did not experience the hardship, you would not have gained the wisdom.

15. Your stressors are survivable. In fact, surviving them makes you stronger.

16. Everything happens *for* you, not to you, and you are least likely to see that in the moment.

17. Resiliency and discipline are the two most integral components to seeing success in your life, whether that be personally or professionally.

18. You never gave up on yourself, stuck true to your vision, and leaned on your moral compass when you knew you were losing your grip.

19. Without peace, there is no power, and without power, there is no **freedom**.

20. Stop being your own worst enemy.

Most of all, I would tell you that you are loved.

That you are understood and that you did the best you could. That you did not have it easy by any means, and that your feelings were valid. That the mistakes were not avoidable because without them, you could not have known better now. That I forgive you and that I commend you for surviving the torrential downpours.

SELF-CARE

Self-care is more than just bubble baths, face masks, a cup of coffee, and a good massage. It is beyond a night in your pajamas watching your favorite movie with a pint of cookie dough ice cream in hand. It is more than the pampering you indulge in to bring yourself back to a state of tranquility.

Self-care is all about taking care of yourself emotionally, physically, and mentally.

It is all about checking in with yourself often and evaluating what is and is not working. It is placing yourself in relationships that bring out the best in you. It is paying close attention to your inclinations, to who you feel lightest around, and to your needs. More than that, it is consistently *respecting* those needs.

It is, as the word states, fully taking care of yourself. Not just recharging on Sunday because you are so wiped out from the week prior—it is not letting yourself get to that point in the first place.

Understand that you need to look after yourself with the same love and protection you show your family members and peers. That in order to feel happy and content, you need to integrate self-care into your routine on a constant basis (not just when it feels convenient). That the more often you engage in this practice, the more natural it will feel and the less thought you will have to put into taking exquisite care of yourself.

SMALL CIRCLES

U nderstand that quality is far more important than quantity.

You are much better off having a few close, devoted friends who genuinely appreciate and accept you for who you *are* than having a bunch of fake ones who talk behind your back and do not have your best interests at heart.

Please consider the power of small circles, of concentrated, richer ones. Ones that do not make you question your worth, and that bring out the absolute best in you. Circles that empower you to be who you are, unapologetically, and bring you closer to your highest self than you have ever been before. The very circles that do not require you to switch into different versions of yourself just to appease the expectations of others.

Circles that value your inner, most authentic voice and that are not high maintenance.

ENVIOUS

Even when others envy you for being brave enough to step into your truth, I hope you continue being the bigger person.

I hope that when others show you the worst of themselves, you consistently show them the best version of you. I hope that when the world seems like it is totally against you, you do not turn against yourself. When others act with malice, bitterness, and jealousy in their hearts, continue to be kind because the world does not need any more negative energy.

It does not need more mean or hurt. It needs more genuineness, more people who are so established in who they are that they do not feel the need to stoop to the level of their counterparts. It needs more people who know that other people's hate is not about them: it is more so about their insecurities and lack of self-love. They are intelligent enough to notice that they are not the issue. **They are sensible enough to know that the issue is the *other person*.**

Remember that no matter how hard you work towards your objectives, someone is going to have something nasty or oppositional to say about you. Someone will do everything they can to drag you through the mud.

It does not matter as long as you keep working on yourself, for yourself. As long as you steer clear of envy.

FLYING BY

The older you get, the more ventures you take part in, the more responsibilities, chores, and deadlines you acquire, and the faster time moves by.

Weeks blur into months, and then into years, and then into strings of time. It all becomes one fast-paced, never-ending blob of monotony—the same mornings, workdays, and hustle. You find yourself asking where the days went, or how you missed the conference, brunch, or birthday party, when really, **you were so bound up in your to-do list that you could not see *out*.**

Then, when you pack a side hustle, committed relationship, new hobby, family obligation, master's degree, or personal transformation onto your plate, you start to get really overwhelmed. You start questioning your priorities and asking yourself which behaviors, actions, and people you could easily go without.

Know that reaching this place is monumental because it is in this moment when you realize that it is less about *shaping* your life to look a certain way, and more about *living* your life in that way. That it does not matter what you fill your time with—it is whether the things you fill your time with add value. Whether they teach, mold, and motivate you to become the human being you know you are capable of actualizing.

It is more about making conscious efforts to slow down, rest, and breathe, than it is about moving a million miles an hour in hopes of getting your goals crossed off faster.

INQUISITIVE

I hope you know that as you become physically and mentally transformed, people will notice—and that you cannot blame them. A shift in your appearance, character, and the way you carry yourself is noticeable. Human beings, by nature, are curious, and they want to know what you are doing differently to become such a better, healthier, smarter version of yourself.

They will expect you to give them a whole spiel about dieting or about paying a bunch of money to learn how to become well again. Little do they know that all you are doing is digging deep into yourself. Little do they know that all the acts you take, and all the ideas you have taught yourself, are available to you for free. **And that they are available to them for free, too.**

I hope you remember that even as your friends and family members inquire about your reinvention, you do not need to let their statements determine the way you feel about yourself. You do not need to let them rock you.

Know that when you filter out snarky comments from ones that are reassuring and celebratory, you will no longer feel the need to prove or explain yourself to anyone. You will not tolerate any disrespect or vacillate from your mission.

You are ready to oversee the questions that will unavoidably come your way.

REPETITION

U nderstand that repeating yourself is not going to make some-one understand you. You could repeat yourself a hundred times, but if the person you are speaking with is incapable of com-prehending what you have to say, **you will spend your entire life translating your soul into an unfamiliar language.**

Your time will be consumed with properly wording your feelings, tippy-toeing around the elephant in the room, and putting another person's emotional immaturity ahead of your own mental health. Your energy will be so drained petitioning for someone else's un-derstanding that you will have none left to acknowledge how your actions endanger your well-being.

Know that if you need to tell someone how to make you feel, they are not the right person for you. Once you try to instruct some-one how to think, you will soon realize that their natural thought process does not align with yours. You will also realize that reaching common ground is nearly impossible because the other person does not possess the propensity to empathize with your point of view. Thus, you will continue to feel let down each time they promise to change. You will keep getting tossed around, taken advantage of, and stepped on.

You will keep feeling these things because you tolerate them.

By keeping your dictionary handy and constantly pacifying con-versations through converting your emotions into digestible, bite-sized chunks, you diminish yourself. You lose yourself to a person who is not right for you, and is not capable of becoming right for you, either.

PAUSING

Wherever possible, take a full day for yourself. Pause.

Whether that means working harder on the weekend to be able to take a weekday off school or using your paid time off on a self-care day. Whether that means dropping your baby off at your mom's house so that you can have time to unwind and relax.

Whatever steps you need to take, I hope you promise yourself that you will catch your breath. Slow down, celebrate the wins, and recuperate. Give yourself the opportunity to reflect.

Remember that these acts are essential components of your assemblage, and that if you do not respect them as such, you will become *deficient* in them. As a result, you will never operate at your highest potential.

Please make the time. Commit yourself to pausing, no matter what it takes.

SELF-MASTERY

Self-mastery: mastering the art of understanding who you are.

Self-mastery is a gift. It is a reward you get for putting in resolute, consistent effort. For becoming your own biggest fan. Self-mastery is what you get for keeping your eyes wide open as you hit mile markers and not just fixating on the finish line. It is what you get for changing your lifestyle to ensure your alterations remain permanent. It is what you get for searching for validation within yourself before petitioning for validation from another. Finally, it is what you get for awakening your inner voice, shutting out the noise, and actualizing your highest self.

SUPPORTERS

I hope you stop normalizing the concept that you cannot do what you want unless you have the support of others.

I hope you stop holding yourself back to let other people's lights illuminate the night sky.

I hope you stop accommodating for others to make them feel more secure about themselves.

I hope you stop convincing yourself that unless you win other people's approval, you will never succeed.

I hope you stop downplaying your potential to keep yourself in your comfort zone—since that is the only place you have ever felt loved.

I hope you stop making fun of yourself before anyone else gets the chance to do so.

Because these actions will get you nowhere. *Nowhere.*

You must vacate the beliefs of people who do not understand the true you because their opinions are uninformed and too hefty to carry. In a journey that stands on the pillars of lightness and happiness, understand that heaviness does not have a place to breed.

You must also believe that you can accomplish whatever you set your mind to, whether you have one person backing you, or fifty people, or zero people. You must stop allowing the support of strangers, colleagues, and friends to dictate your willingness to try new things—to start that business, to go back to school... to retrieve your inner voice.

TUNNEL VISION

I f you have tunnel vision—if all you do is zero in on the negatives, losses, and failures—know that you will never find your WHY. That you will get lost behind all the sadness and intrusive thoughts.

Disappearing into this tunnel of dense fog is not synonymous with evolution, though. Because of this fact, I need you to put your window wipers on full blast and clear out the dampness. I need you to assign meaning to your judgments in ways that help you the next time around. To applaud the moments when you pushed through, especially when you did not think you could.

Remember that you owe it to yourself to make your mind an inviting and calming place to be—not one that spoils your peace and leaves you empty inside.

WANTS VERSUS WISHES COMPLEX

I want you to know that unless you genuinely want something, you are probably just wishing it into existence.

A wish is something that you would love to happen. It is also something that you are not going to take many steps towards actualizing.

Know that unless you are actively working towards whatever it is you *"wished"* you had—a less stressful job, a six-pack, a healthier relationship—then you are not going to make any progress at all. Unless you are fostering a mindset of optimism, as opposed to a mindset of pessimism, you will fail to push forward on arduous days.

I hope you remember that without concentrated efforts, nothing comes of your dreams. You spend your time *talking*, but not *doing*, yet doing is the most vital part of result generation.

Now that you understand the difference between wishing for something and wanting something, you can make educated strides towards turning your wishes into permanent wants. Wants that you constantly have top of mind and that spur your inquisitiveness. Wants that teach you about yourself, what makes you tick, and how to restore your glow.

It is in the transition from turning your wishes into wants that you bloom.

CONDITIONED

H ave you realized that you have been conditioned to behave a certain way from the moment you were born?

- That the way your parents talked about money impacted the
  way you saw the *importance* of money?

- That the punishment and embarrassment you were subject to
  as a child has lingered in the back of your mind for years and
  years and years?

- That the emotions you bottled up and buried under the rug are
  now fuming out of you at lightning speed? That they are alter-
  ing the way you respond to the present moment and tarnishing
  you in every way possible?

- That the friends you surround yourself with—especially the
  ones who are insecure themselves, use toxic coping methods,
  and do not stop calling you for advice—influence your own
  behavior?

- That your counterparts dictate your outlook on life, where you
  want to live after graduation, who you think is attractive, and
  what you think is cool?

Once you recognize these conditions, you can do something
about them because you are in control of your energy, philosophies,
and context. You can remain conscious of your ecosystem and unpack behaviors that are not compatible with your new narrative.

HABITS

In case you did not realize this already, your habits decide your future. **Not the other way around.**

Your habits are a direct indicator of how your future will play out, so please prioritize healthy habits above all else.

Commit to finding patterns that work with your schedule and that make you feel better about yourself. Dedicate your time to activities that make you feel alive and not to ones that drown your energy. Continue going to the gym to get in the shape of your dreams. Make it a priority to work on your side hustle or to finish that craft that has been waiting for you in your drawer. Strongly consider setting systems in place that make your habits easier to maintain, because although you have the best intentions, there will be days when you do not feel inspired. Having a system to simplify things, instead of complicating them, will be your saving grace in these moments.

You decide what your habits are, but at the end of the day, they decide where you end up years down the line.

BEST SELF

When you find your patience being tested, and do not know which place to turn to next, ask yourself how the best version of yourself would manage whatever you are facing right now.

How would she react and what would she say to the person who is bothering you right now? To the friend who broke your trust? To the family member who made a mistake and hurt your feelings? How would she face that person?

My guess is that she would be kind. **That she would remember that being the bigger person is far more important than proving a point.**

Remember that you carry yourself with so much grace and confidence. That you should speak up for yourself and assert your worth, but that there is no need to argue with people who are not at your level. No matter how eloquently, seriously, and loudly you try to illustrate your point, they will never get what you are saying if it is out of their realm of understanding. They will never get it if it is not something they are willing to put the time into understanding, either.

They are not on the same level as you and they do not care enough to get to that level. *You will be wasting your breath and time.*

When you find your patience being tested and do not know which place to turn to next, I hope your strategy is rooted in how the highest version of yourself would face turmoil and present herself.

INDEPENDENT FEMALES

Independent females are to be worshiped.

Independent females should be held in the highest regard because they are the ones who do not question doing their own thing, on their own time, *by themselves.*

The ones who could care less what strangers think of them or say about them because they know that those individuals do not know their story. That they could never understand who they truly are, so therefore their opinions and statements are completely unfounded. *Why sweat over them?*

Independent females are the ones who know their worth.

They are so confident in themselves, in their vision, and in their purpose that they do not feel overly attached to anyone or anything.

They do not need unending strings of compliments to feel secure.

They do not need male attention to feel beautiful.

They do not need phony friends in their lives to lift them up and motivate them to be the best version of themselves.

They are so intensely rooted in their identity that they do not compare themselves to others. They do not need someone else to carry them through life. To pay their bills. To style their hair, wash their clothes, or cook them dinner every night. *They thrive on their own.*

While they appreciate and enjoy the company of loved ones, they know that regardless of another person's presence, life moves on. And they will move on because they have themselves, and **that is all they truly need.**

KISS YOUR SAFETY ZONE GOODBYE

Whichever decision evokes the most fear within you is the one that you need to make.

That is the one that you need to make because that is the one that teaches you the most. That is the decision that helps you become the highest version of yourself, and it is also the one that you need to overcome the most.

Remind yourself that ignoring your fears only exacerbates them. That if you overlook your fears, you prevent yourself from entering a new level of consciousness.

Please address the fear that afflicts you when you sleep at night, when you gaze out the train window, and when you evaluate your life's direction. Kiss your safety zone goodbye.

GRACIOUS

G ratitude. *"The quality of being thankful; readiness to show appreciation for and to return kindness"* (Oxford Languages).

Gratitude is instrumental to your wellness journey. When you find opportunities to show appreciation for the things in your life, you become much more aware of the goodness surrounding you. Instead of reverting to the discords, to what did not go your way, to your losses, and to the things that bother you, you make it a priority to see things in an optimistic light. You never take your parents, partner, and closest friends for granted. You know that without them, you could never be who you are today.

That without their support and love, you would be incomplete.

RIDE THE WAVE

R ide the wave.

Sit with your feelings instead of automatically running away from them. Let your emotions submerge you. Let them soak into every organ in your body and impact your mind, challenge your thoughts, and stimulate your heart.

Know that letting your feelings exist is much more difficult than shutting them out—that it does not take much to pretend that they are not there and function as if everything is okay when you know it is not. Permitting your emotions to speak, however, takes a lot of effort.

When you are strong enough to sit with your feelings, though, you are strong enough to *defeat* them. You are strong enough to face the root of them—the traumas, bad memories, and pain. You are strong enough to handle and exterminate them as well.

You wind up much farther along than you would have if you kept wading back and forth in the current. Than if you never weeded through your layered dimensions and refused to evaluate all your emotions regardless of whether they scared or enraged or enthralled you.

MASTER YOUR MOOD

M aster your mood because your emotions have an enormous hold on you.

When you are **stressed**, you likely struggle to concentrate. You feel flustered and overwhelmed. You feel like you are drowning in work, deadlines, and a never-ending stream of irritation. Your head hurts and you cannot eat without feeling nauseous.

When you are **disappointed**, your heart feels like it is being crushed. You feel like you are not good enough and like you do not have what it takes to win over the people you wish you could win over the most. You feel discouraged, sad, and hurt.

When you are **embarrassed**, you struggle to look other people in the eye. You are not confident in who you are or in what you stand for. You do not want to face the world because you cannot face *yourself*.

The worst part about these feelings is that far too often, you find yourself feeling them because of the insignificant, rude, calculated actions of other people. Their demeanor seriously affects you; it brings you down to your lowest self.

Therefore, it is essential that you take the time to comprehend your moods. That you regain control of yourself to the point that no matter what anyone else has to say about you, you are okay.

Remind yourself that you are in command of your existence.

GATEKEEPER

In a highly digitized world where everyone has something to say about *everything*, I hope you take back control by deliberately improving your content diet.

If you find yourself feeling incredibly stressed and upset after you look at your phone, you need to stop asking what is wrong with *you* and start asking what is wrong with your *feed*.

Who or what is making you feel a certain way and why is it getting to you so much? Why do you feel so persuaded to act on-trend? Is it peer pressure? Is it a bunch of outside voices?

When you have the answers to these types of inquiries, you can take strategic action. You can unfollow or mute accounts that do not make you feel seen, heard, or respected. You can set limitations on how often you view certain apps or content sources. You can rearrange your home screen so that your social media does not pop up center stage, too. You can exit the void of endless scrolls.

Remember: it is on you to be the gatekeeper of your own world.

UNEARTHING GEMS

I hope you remind yourself that your self-assembly is all about unearthing the gems lodged deep beneath your surface. That you are not the equivalent of a missing sock that your puppy secretly stuffed underneath your bed because **your highest self is already within you**. She is not missing. *She is just hiding.*

She is hiding under all the weight you carry. Under the weight of other people's ill-advised comments. Crushed by the weight of your finances. Disguised by the weight of stereotypes and false labels. Misguided by the weight of your perceptions. She is concealed by the connotations that have been ingrained into your belief system from day one.

Know that self-assembly is simply about unearthing the gems buried underneath all that weight and noise. That it forces you to become more of yourself than ever before. That it compels you to become the woman you have always been—the one who urgently needs liberation and acceptance.

DISINFECTING

One day, it will all click inside of you: unless you allow yourself to deal with other people's fakeness or meanness, you will not have to deal with other people's fakeness or meanness. *How insane is that?*

You can stop caring tonight. You can stop entertaining bad vibes, negative energy, and outright disrespect today. It does not have to happen *"someday"* when things are in a better place, and you have moved away for college, and it is easier to break ties.

You can start today because all you need to do is reach your limit.

All you need to do is tell yourself that enough is enough. That there is absolutely no need to pollute your world with garbage that oozes into your soul and makes you feel lost.

Removing this trash sanitizes your world—it is like taking household cleaner and disinfecting your space. It ensures that the things in your universe meet expectations, and it also abolishes what is not meant for you.

H2O

I know you have probably heard this before, but just to reiterate, **drinking water is beyond important.**

If you want to feel energized throughout your workday and avoid dozing off during important calls, you need to stay hydrated. If you want to consistently work out at seven o'clock in the morning, you need to hydrate well before you get to the gym. If you want to have the energy to coach your son's soccer game, cook dinner for date night, and walk around the mall with your friends, you need to drink water.

No matter what you want to do, I can assure you that drinking water is vital.

Therefore, I challenge you to think about your liquid intake. To remind yourself that pounding back tequila shots every weekend and not getting enough sleep drains all your energy. To recognize that it leaves you in couch potato mode, which is okay every once in a while (we are all human), but making this a regular thing is detrimental. Repeatedly ordering a massive diet soda at the pizza store is also not a smart decision, because it is packed full of artificial ingredients.

Please drink more water so that you have the fuel to show up as your highest self every single day.

UNCERTAINTY OR CERTAIN MISERY

The way I see it, there are two roads you can travel down: **uncertainty, or** *certain misery*.

The best part about these two choices is that the decision is completely in your hands.

Certain misery is the safest option for those who loathe the unknown. It is for those who would rather suffer in their comfort zone and remain in the same unhappy place their entire life than welcome unfamiliarity. This destination loves people who do not want to risk losing what they have, mortifying themselves, or messing up. Certain misery is what happens when you actively pick actions, habits, routines, and ties that are not in your best interests while concurrently *knowing* they are not in your best interests. It is selecting them because fear paralyzes you and security blindfolds your wandering eyes.

Then, there is uncertainty. There is a road full of unpredictable and unexplainable events. A life in which you cannot know what will happen to you because you are too busy living to worry. You are too consumed in the now to extrapolate into the future.

Choosing to live with uncertainty, instead of with certain misery, almost assures your happiness because no matter what life brings, you are in charge. You are emboldened to navigate the currents and sail whichever way suits you as opposed to miserably waiting at your mooring and never taking off in the first place.

SELF-DISCOVERY

You need to keep pushing. Not for a better friend, a new body, or a dinner plan in the city so you do not have to spend another night alone.

You need to keep pushing to awaken your highest self.

You need to keep pushing to reinvent yourself. To chase your dreams, discover your calling, and embark on unmapped paths. You need to keep pushing to bring new passions and hobbies into your life.

You need to celebrate who you are above all else. You need to venture into the unknown as well, because it is in this unmarked territory that you generate your principles. It is in this place that the possibilities remain endless, and that unique visions are produced.

Thus, I hope you engage in self-discovery because the connection you have with yourself comes before all else. It comes before your job, love, and family. It comes before all these things because you cannot show up for anything or anyone until you show up for yourself.

WELL-READ

A well-read woman is a dangerous and intimidating one.

Now for a moment, consider the possibility that this statement is true.

That voraciously reading ten, twenty, thirty pages a day augments your value. That it causes you to see the universe in a different light because you will have led hundreds of lives in your lifetime, whereas a nonreader will have only led *one*.

That when you engage in literature, you step into an unconventional universe. That if the author excels in his or her craft, he or she can make you feel as if you are one with their primary character and able to understand their circumstances and social status. That you can be teleported back in time, ascribe associations between your favorite characters' actions and your own, expand your vocabulary, and adopt a rare affiliation for language itself, all based on the pearls of wisdom embedded within the text.

Now that you have considered this to be true, I hope you see how being a well-read woman may very well turn you into a threat (especially to those who do not value reading or see the purpose in growth). How it will frighten those who fear your knowledge because they know that you are thriving while they are too busy making excuses for why they cannot flourish themselves.

MIND GAMES

You cannot believe everything your mind thinks.

Know that if you find yourself running away into a river of anxiety at the precipice of one single thought, the issue is not your mind itself, but your *reaction* to the content it produces. That until you get a firm grasp over your brain and accept the fact that thoughts will randomly arise from your subconscious—regardless of whether they should be rationalized into existence and paid attention to—you will continue to suffer.

You will never be able to regain control over your headspace because you never accepted the fact that you lost control in the first place. **Your mind will enslave you because you have yet to reclaim your inner voice.**

THIS YEAR

Maybe this year is all about taking back what was yours to begin with.

So tell yourself that this year will be different. That this will be the year that changes everything. It will be the year that you drop the labels, love yourself, and embrace authenticity. The one where you try new foods, join an intramural league, and tap into the passion that has been whispering in your ear. The very year that you reconnect with the woman who already exists within your strong bones, radiant soul, and glowing heart.

Just get out there and start because this year is all about becoming more of yourself than you ever *allowed* yourself to be before. It is the year you become the person you know you were always meant to be—the one who lives her truth and is not afraid anymore. The year you become restored and reborn.

ON DECK

When I wake up before the sun rises, I cannot help but fantasize about what the day holds in store for me. Not what *I* hold in mind for the day, but what the day has on deck for *me*.

I know that despite the vision I set forth for the day, life will happen. It may start raining as soon as I set out to walk during my lunch break. I may have to rearrange my schedule. Reading tonight may be a no-go because I will get a call from someone I have not spoken to in a while, and we will get caught up. I might rethink skipping my workout this evening because I feel bloated and lazy and need a way to exert my energy.

Please understand that the forces and happenings of your life are not chance occurrences: they all have meaning. Thus, I need you to pay attention to natural cues and to stop going about your days as you would regardless of whether they presented themselves.

Know that you owe it to yourself to appreciate the world around you. To treat each sunrise and sunset as bookends to start fresh, as markers to reinvent yourself and live your truth.

BASELINE

You need to know the person you are working with today before you can become the person you aspire to be tomorrow. **You need a baseline.**

When you are so busy chasing external feats, attention, and influence, however, you can never understand yourself because your energy is being mismanaged entirely.

Remember that you must install components that align with your inner voice, and designate your baseline, before you can push anyone or anything else to fit into your world.

INFORMATION GAPS

I f there is ever an argument that wins you over, I think it should be this one: **you did the best you could given what you knew at the time.**

You were just a kid who was starting to understand the world. You were just stepping into your identity, figuring out what you stood for, and determining where you fit into this chaotic universe.

Think about how much you had on your plate at that time. Reflect on how much you were battling and how hard you were trying to keep your head above water. *How could you possibly have known any better than you did?*

Accept that you could not have known any better back then, thus you did what any person would naturally do: you fought for your survival. Now that you made it out to the other side, though, you have taken the time to learn from your shortcomings and implement steps to avoid making the same mistakes twice.

Know that it is time to accept your own forgiveness because you have plugged your information gaps. And yes, while I know this is the hardest forgiveness to bestow, and that you are so used to being your own biggest critic, I also know that once you exonerate yourself, you can move forward.

HUNGER

Something I have learned in my twenty-two years of life that I think defines all evolution: **if you want it badly enough, your hunger will find a way to make it happen.**

If you want it badly enough, you will *put it* into existence. The sacrifices needed to get an extra hour of sleep each night will come naturally, whether they include not being able to hang out with your friends, turning off your phone, or setting stiffer boundaries. You will adjust your routine so that going to the gym three times a week is easier. You will opt for buying meal kits so that when it comes time for dinner you are excited to cook (and not Googling the menu for your favorite Thai spot). Making excuses for yourself will end, and so will accepting failures as defining moments.

You will stop allowing fear to rule over your life and you will stop holding yourself back because when you want it badly enough, *you find a way.*

The only way to know that you did not want it that badly is to locate when you found a reason not to act. If you found a way to rationalize why you could not do what was necessary to make something realistic, you did not have hunger because with hunger, nothing is too scary, too much, or too long—it is all part of satisfying your unquenchable appetite.

UNAVAILABLE

Your entire life shifts the moment you accept the fact that unavailability is a good thing.

That not being instantly accessible to all your friends, family members, and colleagues forces them to respect your time. That placing consistent boundaries around your expectations gives you the energy you so desperately need. That decreasing your availability ensures that you fill yourself up *before* spending all your efforts and love on others, too.

Please stop viewing being available to the people in your life 24/7 as a good thing because all it does is drain you. It is the cause of your frustration and stress because when you are overly available to another person, job, or peer, you will be taken for granted. People will know that they can suck the life out of you because you will always stay. You will always put in the extra work and never say no. As a result, society chips away at you and brings you a deep hurt.

It is time to embrace being unavailable.

THE TAKER

The ultimate energy taker: an extremely **cluttered** and **disorganized** space.

Your environment is a direct reflection of your potential. Not just in people terms, but in physical space terms, too. If you live in a messy room where everything is all over the place, your bed is never made, your empty water bottles litter the floor—and you keep tripping over last night's outfit and your spare change—then your life will follow a similar beat.

You will feel all over the place and unkempt. You will feel like you cannot catch your step because you are always falling over something.

When you feel off **internally**, there is an **external** link.

1. Did you clean your room today?

2. Did you make it a point to clear off your desk, fold your laundry, and donate clothes you no longer wear?

3. Did you spray your favorite perfume and open the windows to air out your space and get it smelling nice and fresh again?

4. Did you declutter?

5. Did you throw out the pen that exploded while you were finishing your calculus homework last night?

6. Did you get rid of the wrappers (and the empty water bottles) scattered about?

THE PROTOTYPE

It is crucial to align your actions and mindset with the actions and mindset of someone you would want to look up to.

Behave in the same way you would want someone who looks up to *you* to behave because the world is always watching. Whether you are aware of it or not, there are people in this world who think you are fantastic. Who admire your courage and think highly of you. They wonder how you make it look so effortless and how you have it all together, even when you may disagree with them yourself.

Some of your biggest cheerleaders are anonymous, and if anything, this should prove to you how impactful your patterns are. You are ultimately teaching those who look up to you, who see you as a marvelous prototype, how to act *themselves*.

Promise yourself that you will always act with integrity and benevolence because someone has their eye on you, and you do not even know it yet.

STOP SETTLING

Stop settling.

When there is a voice urging you to chase your dreams, listen to it. When you wake up feeling gloomy in the morning, unsure of how you got to this point, lift yourself up instead of accepting it for what it is.

Stop being a stranger in your own world because it is beyond tiring.

Stop settling for relationships that do not give you joy, support, and enthusiasm. Terminate partnerships that do not fulfill all the things you need them to. Quit compromising for friends who talk behind your back, for jobs you dislike but pay the bills—for anything below expectations that makes you feel like you got the short end of the stick.

Also, know that the only person who can halt your settling tendencies is yourself. That until you tell yourself that there is no way you can continue accepting things that do not match up with your lifestyle, aspirations, and ambitions, you will remain stuck.

Please pursue whatever you genuinely want in life with arms wide open because even if you fail, you will fail much farther along than you would have if you never stopped settling.

PART 5

POLISHING

POLISHING

The final stage.

Polishing is all about ensuring your changes are sustainable. It is also about making sure your home is well-decorated and wholesome.

During this period of transformation, cementing an indestructible house is pivotal because as your life goes on, different obstacles will challenge your willpower. They will uncover the legitimacy of your transformation by showing you whether it is secure enough to withstand disturbances and heartbreaks. These times will reveal whether you really love yourself enough to get back up when you fall. They will show you whether you know who you are and whether your habits, systems, rituals, and affirmations can stand the test of time.

Know that while polishing is the end of this growth cycle, it is only the *beginning* of your personal development. That when one chapter of evolution closes, another one inevitably opens. That being elastic and fine-tuning as you go is a must.

Please take all the lessons from this transformation and apply them to adverse periods that will emerge in the future because education is the bedrock of growth.

QUITTING

The only way to fail is to quit entirely.

When you ask yourself why you are so nervous about getting started in the first place—and the fear of failure comes gleaming through—I hope you actively remind yourself that you will not fail unless you let yourself fail. Unless you completely give up and allow yourself to fall into an elusive hole of nothingness.

Please know that the fact that you have read this collection up until this point shows that you will not fail because you *care*. And when you care, you do not give up: you get inventive, and you find a way. You may pivot along the way, too, but this is also not synonymous with failure because giving up on one route to pursue one that is more aligned with who you are means you self-educated, stayed true to yourself, and found a better way to reach the same goal.

Maybe it is time to take back your power because the only way you can possibly fail is if you stop trying altogether.

PERSEVERANCE

Your discipline will constantly be tested.

There will be days when the last thing you want to do is rise in the morning and give it another go. Days when a life of greed, angst, and pleasure sound much more appealing than continuing to do deep work on yourself.

As I keep saying—it is not easy. Yet, the journey you have embarked on signifies one of the most important steps you have taken in your life. This assemblage has taught you more about yourself than you could ever imagine. About the heart that keeps you fueled to tackle each day. About the arms that carry the weight of the world and the ears that have heard every negative word in the dictionary uttered in association with your name, but still seek happiness.

Know that your brain, soul, and voice did not become themselves overnight. That they have been hardened by your circumstances, by the events that have shaped, altered, and distracted your vision. Remember that unlearning can be just as important as learning about yourself in times of change, and that although you will continue to be tested, you will survive.

Now that you have been in the unknown for long enough, you have no other option but to persevere—to become the person you daydream about.

OVERTHINKING

Overthinking will ruin any chance you have at functioning on a high level. It will make you feel like there is constantly another thought to tend to because when you overthink, there *always is* another thought to tend to.

Your mind churns out ideas, one after the next, while hardly giving you a second to understand each one. Overthinking causes chaos within your soul, too. It encourages you to form elongated projections of what *could* be happening, or why he *may* be upset at you, or whether your interviewer *possibly* thought you were lame instead of looking at the truth of the matter.

Understand that overthinking incapacitates you. It makes it hard for you to interact, go about your days with peace of mind, and sleep for eight-plus hours.

If your brain is overactive—repeatedly thinking of a new sport to try, a new business to create, or a next blog post to write—please take deliberate efforts to subdue your production line. Incorporate mindset habits that allow you to find the off switch (and then actually press the button and shut off your brain). Doing this helps you recapture control of your perception and your own potential because when you force yourself to discard nonsensical thoughts and trudge forward, you get closer and closer to the light and farther and farther from overthinking.

TREATMENT

A universal truth: **the way you treat others comes back to you tenfold.** Please be aware of your manners and actions, and of the energy you put into the atmosphere.

Know that stealing a yogurt from the store instead of paying for it at the self-checkout booth will return to you. Rolling your eyes at the store clerk who does not speak English and needs to call a manager over to process your refund will, too. Cheating on your significant other will return to you as well—and so will not being true to who you are (the biggest energy waster of all).

You will feel it in the way you walk, in the way you talk, and in the opportunities that the universe pushes into your life. Likewise, you will feel it in your own self-image.

The opposite is also true, though.

Holding the door for a stranger in a wheelchair will return to you. Donating your old clothes to the poor instead of selling them will return to you. Taking time to explain a system to a new employee at your company will return to you, as will giving others the gift of knowing your highest self.

It is all an interconnected loop.

GOSSIP

You need to be careful about who you share your thoughts with. Be intentional about who you open up to because everyone promises that they will never tell. Everyone swears that it will stay between you and them, and you and them *only*. Everyone wants in on the secrets, betrayals, and juice. They feast off the lies and the heartbreak.

When you confide in someone, I hope you ask yourself whether you should unpack your feelings onto them.

- Will they really have your back if things go south?

- If you quit being friends, partners, or peers, will they blab your stories to the world or will they honor their word?

- Are they worth spending time speaking with, or would you be better off journaling?

Understand that not everyone is worth your breath.

Some things are better left unsaid, especially to not-so-trustworthy people. You will save yourself a lot of stress and backtracking if you do not open your mouth in the first place because not everyone has the same heart as you. Not everyone thinks twice before crossing a person they gave their word to because we are not all built the same.

GRAYSCALE

F inding the space between giving it your all and giving it nothing.

Between pouring your heart out in hopes of forming meaningful connections and withholding any sign of emotion because you cannot bear to be let down again.

The space between laughing and crying, failing and climbing, and punishing and clapping exists, but when you are socially conditioned to see the world as a pole and its antipode, you cannot see the grayscale.

The grayscale, **the space between**, forgoes extremes. It is an undefined territory we often overlook. One that seems so far removed from reality but really contains immense power.

ALONE

Intentionally choose to stop fearing alone time.

Love the intimate moments you spend with yourself—like when you are showering off after sitting on the beach all day and getting dressed in your favorite dinner outfit. Or when you are snuggled up on the couch with a magazine. When you are walking down the street making returns, running errands, buying gifts for friends, or prepping for a get-together.

Look forward to nights by yourself. Look forward to cooking yourself dinner and ending the evening with a movie. Enjoy writing, exercising, walking, and taking care of your body in the way your *specific body* needs to be taken care of (you are a houseplant, remember?). More than anything else, learn to embrace your time alone and use it to your advantage.

Be much more calculated about how you spend your time and tend to your needs.

Fill yourself up first. Parade around your living room and wake yourself up with a splash of cold water. Whatever you need to do, please rid yourself of the fear of being in your own skin, on your own time, without anyone or anything else to entertain you.

You are more than fine by yourself because you can be anyone you want to be.

RESPECT

S o many of the world's issues do not stem from politics. They do not stem from opposing world powers, leaders of government, corporate America, or public institutions and administrations, either. **They stem from a lack of respect for different opinions and lifestyles.**

In a world full of billions of people, know that there is absolutely no way we could all agree. It is not possible because of unique social conditionings and upbringings. Until you stop believing that your mind is responsible for rearranging the world to make it suitable for your own threshold, for fixing your inner problems by changing something outside of you, you will continue scouring for a resolution that is never going to surface. Thus, it is less about *blaming* the world you live in for weighing you down, and more about asking yourself how you can do better *given* the uncontrollable.

- How can you accept others' faults?

- How can you uplift as opposed to ridiculing, blaming, and judging?

- How can you celebrate another person's success without questioning your own?

- How can you maximize what you have instead of lamenting over what you do not?

- How can you express sincere happiness for others instead of resenting them for doing and being and living in a way that is *"better"* than yours?

Understand that your solution is to stop holding so much disdain for the life you are living and to start looking for ways to be the best version of yourself. To incorporate respect into your daily practices and embrace differences as **learning** points instead of as **pain** points. To consistently show up as your highest self, and to release your mind from its duties of making the irrepressible world a better place for you to live in and repairing what is wrong inside of you.

COMPLAINTS

I f you catch yourself whining every single time you come home from school, or from your job, or after your long commute, you have two options.

First, you can keep doing exactly what you are doing and continue complaining about it all the time. This routine resembles the exact definition of insanity: doing the same thing and expecting different results.

Or you can eliminate the thing you are complaining about and replace it with something that better serves your needs.

The thing is, though, if you are a chronic complainer—if you find a way to dislike anything put in front of you—you will *always* locate a disturbance. You will always identify what you do not like about the next major, the next opportunity, the next partnership, and the next pet.

If this sounds like you, know that the problem is not *what* you have in your life, but *how* you allow it to control you. **The problem is your reaction to those things.**

Instead of hating your time at your current gig, I challenge you to think of ways to enhance your days while still being at that place. Go for a walk during your lunch break, use your benefits, and quit checking emails after hours. Think of ways to improve how you are *handling* what you already have, rather than *complaining* your way into a newer, more promising situation.

Understand that you will subject the latest things in your world to the same cynical outlook you have on life itself. You will keep moaning about everything that enters your universe unless you fix your headspace first.

CHARACTER VERSUS REPUTATION

There is a stark difference between your **character** and your **reputation**.

Your character is how you act every single day. It is how you lead your life, the person you bring forth into the world each morning, and your likes and dislikes. **It is who you are.**

Your reputation, however, is much different than your character. You can be a solid, strong, happy person, and you can still have a poor reputation in the eyes of someone who is jealous of you.

Understand that your reputation solely consists of what *other people* think of you. It is a product of their impressions and opinions, yet there can be no truth or weight to their perspective because when someone does not know you, they cannot possibly make a precise judgment.

If someone tries to tarnish your reputation and makes you feel self-conscious, please ask yourself if their opinions are valid and if they know you well enough to brand you.

Distinguishing between these two concepts is important because when you enable someone else's vision of you to define your character, you wander further and further away from your highest self.

PHYSICALITY

When your eyes are always zeroed in on physical results, **you lose yourself.**

You lose yourself by constantly watching your body in the mirror and feeling dissatisfied with your reflection. By disrupting your own body image. You lose yourself to inescapable, obsessive routines and workouts energized by the nagging chatter inside your head. To the scale, the numbers, the calorie counting, the macros, and the nutrition labels.

They are all that matter when you are in this trap.

When your eyes are always set on physical progress, you lose sight of what counts. The steps you have already accomplished to get to the place you are today become irrelevant. The journey itself fades into an abyss.

The only way to get out of this cycle is by consciously *preventing* yourself from fixating on end goals. Know that when you are disciplined, the results follow no matter how long it takes. Know that when you are doing what truly makes you happy, any outcome is acceptable because you are enjoying your time reaching that place.

Please stop obsessing over the metrics and outside indicators, and pay more attention to how you feel inside. *That is all that matters.*

CHAOTIC

Chaos is an awakening cloaked as an explosion, but if these concepts are contradictory in your mind, I hope you know that they should be. Society does not permit the idea that madness can be related to wokeness. The two cannot co-exist because they are opposites of one another.

Today, however, I want you to dispel this distinction. Consider the idea that these two poles are far more alike than you ever imagined.

That through the chaos, the scramble, and the disorganization comes the ability to transform. That when things fall apart, they are really falling together in your favor. That eruptions open the possibility for your world to align. That experiencing the loss, embarrassment, and sadness allowed your body to thirst for happiness, love, and companionship more deeply than ever before. That you were given the chance to rewrite your narrative because chaos gave you no other choice *but* to rewrite it.

That maybe chaos can be the start of something glorious. It can open new doors and bring you closer to your ideal self than you have ever been before. Maybe all that is left to do now is to accept this theory as truth and stop rejecting your efforts to advance.

APOLOGIES

Maybe it is time for you to finally apologize to yourself for all the mean, cruel, hurtful things you told yourself over the years.

For not being wise enough to shun the nasty comments your mind whispered in your ear. For crushing your spirits before a colleague, teacher, or boyfriend could do it first. For subconsciously calling yourself fat, ugly, and unattractive whenever you looked in the mirror. And for all the mean things you told yourself under your breath while you scrolled through your social media feed.

Maybe it is time for you to apologize to yourself for holding yourself back.

After your work through all this, it is also time to show forgiveness. To move beyond the mishaps and be okay with the fact that you did not treat yourself kindly in the past. That you destroyed your self-esteem because you were scared.

Know that until you forgive yourself for all the anguish you put yourself through, you will find it impossible to move on. Giving yourself the compassion you deserve allows you to walk with love in your heart. It encourages you to lift yourself up instead of pushing yourself down to the ground. Most of all, it stops you from using your words as weapons.

NOT THAT IMPORTANT

J ust in case you were not already aware, **you are not that important to me.**

Quit fluffing your ego and thinking that you are the center of my universe when in reality, you are a small piece of my existence. *Do I love and care for you with all my heart?* Of course, but will my world be crushed if one day you decide that I am not good enough for you? Absolutely not.

I already know what it feels like to lose myself. I have already broken my own heart, belittled myself, and made myself feel the smallest I have ever felt in my entire life. I have done more damage with my own small hands than your large ones could ever imagine doing to me. So no, you are not that important.

Stop flattering yourself.

I care for you, but you will never be the end of me. Without you, I am still complete. I can still move mountains, hold my head up high, try new things, and adventure. I can be human whether you are in my life or out of it. I can be happy, smell the flowers outside the local market on my coffee run, and glide to the rhythm of my own beat.

Without you, I can take care of and spoil myself.

I have already been the lowest I will ever be. Regardless of whether you opt to stay a part of my universe, I will be okay. I have my own hands to hold, my own goals to actualize, and my own life to live.

Just in case you were not already aware, **you are not that important to me.**

SHAME

"A *painful feeling of humiliation or distress caused by the consciousness of wrong or foolish behavior"* (Oxford Languages).

Shame haunts your memories and embarrasses you in front of your friends and family. It binds you so tightly with its fingers that you cannot seem to get away. It compels you to plead for vindication from your own guilt.

Shame will never award you the forgiveness you seek, though, because shame is an emotion you inflict *upon* yourself.

Understand that there will come a point in your life when you are so tired of feeling ashamed for how you dress, for who you kissed, for the job you took, and for the university you chose to attend against your parents' wishes. When you arrive at this place, you will never feel shameful about anything ever again. You will be sick of shame—so over it that you cannot fathom degrading yourself ever again. You will accept your shortcomings and learn from them instead of letting them soak into your bloodstream and erode your confidence.

Please put shame in its place because it is time to stop antagonizing yourself. Constantly being ashamed of yourself is not a healthy way to exist and it thwarts your progress.

WAITING GAMES

I waited for you.

I waited for you to love me for who I was and accept my weaknesses.

I waited for you to mature, to want a woman like me in your life.

For you to turn the corner, overcome your baggage, and be ready to let love in.

And for all those times you called me in the middle of the night, begging me to stay on the line, I waited.

I waited for you after you ghosted me for weeks and went off the grid.

For you to see my worth and realize what you had in front of you.

I waited for you to tell me that I was enough, for you to improve yourself, get over your traumas, and treat me the way I knew I deserved to be treated.

I waited for you to tell me I looked pretty, to take me out to a fancy dinner, and to share our relationship with your friends and family members.

But now, I am tired of waiting. In fact, I will not wait any longer.

I already have everything I need inside of me. I am not defined by your love, and I refuse to base my own self-worth on your opinions. I can no longer wait my entire life for my mind to face the truth: *I am not right for you.*

I am better off on my own than I am waiting for you to get on a page that you are not capable of reaching.

THANK YOU

Thank you for choosing yourself for the very first time and for taking the leap into the unknown.

You would not have made it here without believing in and loving yourself. So thanks for being your own best friend and for coaching yourself through adversities. Thank you for remaining level-headed and collected, and for prioritizing your values. For moving forward when it felt like the universe was doing everything it could to pull you right back into your old ways. Thanks for knowing what was best for yourself and for running after it with an open heart.

It takes a lot of courage to bet on yourself.

Thank you for showing yourself that you have what it takes to succeed and for reclaiming your inner voice. You have inspired many silent viewers, whether you realize it or not. Thanks for setting the tone for your own life instead of allowing it to be set by the tone of your peers. For being brave enough to look at yourself in the mirror every single day until you fell in love with the reflection staring back at you. *You knew you would reach a place of peace.*

Most of all, thank you for never giving up and for being you. Without you, the world would not be the magnificent place it is today. And a world without you is a world I would not want to live in.

REMAINING HER

Maybe it is less about becoming the highest version of yourself, and more about having the continued confidence to show up as her. Even when you are in an unfamiliar situation, and you do not feel protected, be her. And when other people abhor your decisions, be her. When your subconscious leads you towards perilous choices, be her.

Understand that it is more about remaining consistent in who you *are* than it is about being her when you have the backbone for it. Being her only when it feels most comfortable or right is not enough because there is never going to be a picture-perfect time where things are simple and effortless. It will take concerted efforts to show up as her, especially when your past was filled with not letting her see the light of day.

Remember that the hardest part is letting her be free in a world where everyone has something to say about everyone and everything.

SELF-EVALUATION

While self-evaluation is important regardless of your construction phase, it is *most* important when you are nearing the end of your revamp. During polishing, you can clearly look at yourself, raise provoking inquiries, and decide whether you have completed your objectives. In this period, you can confirm that you acted in accordance with your personality and values. You can identify the components of you that were left in the past and those that you brought forward into the now. Additionally, you can reflect upon your mindset.

If you are feeling overwhelmed by how much has transpired during this growth cycle, know this is a good thing. The fact that there are so many evaluation points funneling through your head means that you gave yourself full permission to bloom. It means that you gave yourself the chance to expand, incorporate meaning into your world, and diversify your interests.

If there is ever a time to log your thoughts and reflect, the *finale* of your growth cycle is the most important time to do so.

WOKE

All my life, I could not see past hardships. I could not answer the riddles, and I could not face myself.

It was only after I shuttered out the uninvited guests roaming around my mind, unhinged, that I gained my sense of self back. That I realized I had a voice, and thoughts, and senses of my own. That I fully understood the damages muting myself for all those lonely years did to me.

I may not be perfect, but at least I woke up from that nightmare and repossessed myself.

WHIFF

I want you to understand that it is okay to be happy for how far you have come but to still feel like you have a long way to go.

Once you get a whiff of what it feels like to work on yourself, you are going to look for ways to develop throughout your life. Know that even if you feel like whatever chapter you have been prioritizing is complete to the best of your ability, life will continue giving you opportunities to transform. Although you may feel the need to initiate another chapter after this one ends, **you are better off that way**.

INTIMIDATION

Come to accept the fact that your progress will intimidate people.

It will scare people because they no longer know how to handle the woman with boundaries. These people will not feel confident sitting next to you anymore because your growth makes them feel nervous and inferior. They cannot accept the fact that the woman who used to let people walk all over her is no longer a doormat. That you know what you want, and that you do not care how uncomfortable or threatening your ambition makes others feel.

I need you to accept the fact that their intimidation has nothing to do with you, and everything to do with them.

Your progress is YOUR progress. It is not done with the intention of servicing anyone or anything else. *You are working on yourself, for yourself.* If people feel intimidated by you, know that it is because they are not secure in themselves. Know that it is because they are jealous that you accomplished something they could not do themselves. It is because they are not happy with their lives, and they do not think it is fair that someone else could evolve when they could not figure out how to escape their own cage.

Stop letting other people's discomfort make you uncomfortable when you fleeing your comfort zone is the only thing they are uncomfortable about.

RECAST

"*G ive (an object) a different form by melting it down and reshaping it*" (Oxford Languages).

After all this time spent extracting, reflecting, and reinventing yourself, I hope that you feel remodeled. I hope that the shifts you have made within yourself encourage like-minded people to enter into your universe so that they can add insights and context. I hope that these shifts feel rewarding, too—that they improve the quality of your well-being, expose you to new viewpoints, and quash any persistent anger or sorrow.

I am sure you remember the hardships you fought your way through, though, even as you sit here in restructured form. Please be proud of yourself for that because I am proud of you for persisting. I know that this is not an easy journey and that not everyone is cut out for this. Many people cannot find it within themselves to self-educate and mature. The fact you even made it to this stage says a lot about you, so thank yourself for giving yourself time to redesign.

DANCER

Soak in all the generosity and goodwill you have brought into this world, and be proud of the sensational feats you have accomplished. Think of how far you have come and how excited the younger version of yourself would be for your accolades.

Turn the gradual wins into big moments. Give yourself a break. Be happy. Dance underneath the sun on a bright and beautiful day. Let the breeze trickle into your soul. Feel the vitamin D absorbing into your body. Be the light.

Most of all, stop passing the sunshine phase and moving right into your next mission.

Know that if you never make it a habit to celebrate yourself, you will get exhausted—always looking for *more, more, more*. If what you have done is never enough, then you will continue chasing yourself down a rabbit hole. You will spin your wheels at full steam until you implode.

If you never give yourself the chance to enjoy your victories, they will never seem important or relevant, either. It will never feel like you are enough. While other people may envy your drive, or laud your work ethic, if you never feel you are enough for yourself, **you will never get out of the confines of going, going, going**.

IMPOSTER

I t is oftentimes when you are closest to the finish line that you want to completely give up. You falter because taking yourself from a world where all your focus is on improving, and then moving into a world where new relationships, careers, and tasks come to fruition, is tricky. Doing so causes you to question whether you can keep up the systems you set in place during your time of deep concentration and internal alignment.

When you stop running so quickly, and it comes time to enjoy living in your highest self's body, you freeze up. Instead of trusting yourself, you may be inclined to quit altogether, thinking that you have already done enough and that you do not deserve happiness.

That you are an imposter in your own skin.

When you move from a period of rapid growth into a period of calmness, know that the most important thing you can do is never turn on yourself. Remember that you earned all your rewards, and they are justified.

RESOURCEFUL

"*Having the ability to find quick and clever ways to overcome difficulties*" (Oxford Languages).

The *"quick"* part of this definition is debatable, but the *"clever"* part is something worth pondering because not all obstacles are created equal. **They do not have the same weight.**

Think of adversities like rocks in your backpack. Visualize tens, even hundreds of these rocks weighing down your bag. They slowly kill your posture and cause you immense distress.

In order to dump some of these rocks on the curb and lessen the load you carry with you every single day, you are going to need to act with a little bit of genius. You will also need long-lasting, creative solutions because patching holes only holds up for so long. Your Band-Aids will peel back, and the rocks will worm their way back into your bag.

Being resourceful enough to solve problems with permanent remedies ensures long-term success because these cures place rocks behind you **forever.**

BULLETPROOF

I f you are not entirely satisfied with where you are right now, I hope you know that it is okay to prolong your efforts. Adjusting as you evolve is okay because waiting a little while longer to close this chapter of growth is not a bad thing.

Yet, for many, there may never be a time you feel totally fulfilled. Society encourages you to constantly improve and get better, shrewder, and tougher. You hear it online, in the classroom, and from your family members.

Learning to be okay with the incremental steps you have taken, and accepting yourself for where you are today, is the only way to unfasten this notion. Your assemblage is meant to last a lifetime, and while I am positive that you will find pockets of peace, know that there will be other unpredictable events in your future: this is the reality of being human.

Remember that leaning into dissatisfaction and making the corrections you need today helps you polish your path. It brings you closer to finishing your home renovations and offers you a framework to apply towards future challenges as well. This practice ultimately leaves you bulletproof because no matter what life brings your way, you possess the courage to reinvent yourself while still loving the core of who you are.

KNOW BETTER = DO BETTER

Now that you know better, it should feel like your life calling is to do better. Like there is no other option but to act on the wisdom you have amassed and live out your highest potential. It should feel like you are regressing as soon as you throw yourself back down into the margins of yesterday.

Know that neglecting to act on your discoveries will leave you feeling deflated. It will also leave you stuck in the same sad place you found yourself in when you lifted yourself off the floor and told yourself that you would be victorious.

Now that you know better, there is no other option but to continue doing better.

SIGNIFICANCE

M aybe your story is not meant to be bogged down underneath all the progress you made. **The steps, challenges, sleepless nights, and battles all have gravity.** They do not deserve to be overlooked and camouflaged because bottling up your truth prevents others from getting to know you. It also inhibits you from completing your assemblage and restoring your inner narrative.

Know that your story has meaning because it is what defines you. It differentiates you from the billions of other people in this world.

Having the courage to use your history to make an impact is bold, so please capitalize on your background by inspiring change in your community and across the globe. Never shy away from telling others who you are and how you feel. *Who you really are and how you really feel.* Stop dodging depth in conversations and harness these moments as opportunities to intimately express yourself.

Just think about it: maybe your story can be the one that motivates a peer who has been struggling with his or her mental health to seek help. Or maybe it can attract a following of fellow warriors. You can start a ripple effect in your area that is so large that it outlives you.

Understand that your legacy is cemented when you are brave enough to *become* significant.

ASSIMILATION

I f there is one final concept that should persuade you to never fear standing out from the crowd, let it be this one: **you will never influence, change, or inspire the world by trying to be just like everyone else**. There is no way to create anything worth paying attention to if you follow in the same steps as those in front of you.

If you want to make something beautiful out of your existence and leave a meaningful footprint, I encourage you to stop assimilating. Take that leap and dive headfirst into the unknown. Draft that book, launch that app, move across the country, and run for mayor in your hometown. Know that having a quirkiness to you is something to celebrate, and that if you are surrounded by people who bully you for it, then they are not the people you need in your life.

Realize that wondering what *could have been* if only you had the courage to act in the moment disheartens you. Hating yourself for not running after what was calling your name all those years stings, too. It is not a burn you want to rebound from, either, because you can easily avoid being stung altogether by actively choosing to do otherwise.

Keep innovating, pushing, and designing because the world will reward you for your contributions. You will feel more fulfilled because of them. **You will be fully assembled because of them.**

ABOUT THE AUTHOR

Victoria Lombardi is the author of *Self-Assembly*, a creative nonfiction collection inspired by the journey of awakening a young woman's highest self. She is a writer, a reader, and a deeply introspective and contemplative human being. Her work focuses on the patterns underlying fostering sustainable personal growth and unearthing one's latent potential. She hopes her prose serves as a catalyst for young women across the globe. In her own words, she says:

"Prioritizing the relationship you have with yourself is one of the boldest, most important decisions you'll ever make in your life. Having the discipline to continuously invest in yourself breaks long-standing barriers within your conscious—ones that reinforce your tendency to ignore your own best interests. To transfer all your energy into people, jobs, and external responsibilities before copiously pouring that same amount of energy into yourself. Assemble an identity that aligns with your most authentic self because you will never influence the world by trying to be just like everyone else."

I am rooting for you throughout all your endeavors. I see your strength, and I admire your willingness to sort out your disjointed components and reclaim your inner voice.

Be sure to connect with me on Instagram and share your favorite essays from this collection (@growthwithvictoria).

Made in the USA
Middletown, DE
06 June 2022